Climate Change and its Causes, Effects and Prediction Series

CONSTRUCTING CLIMATE CHANGE LEGISLATION: BACKGROUND AND ISSUES

CLIMATE CHANGE AND ITS CAUSES, EFFECTS AND PREDICTION SERIES

Global Climate Change
Harace B. Karling (Editor)
2001. 1-56072-999-6

Global Climate Change Revisited
Harace B. Karling (Editor)
2007. 1-59454-039-X

Climate Change Research Progress
Lawrence N. Peretz (Editor)
2008. 1-60021-998-5

Climate Change: Financial Risks
*United States Government
Accountability Office*
2008. 978-1-60456-488-4

**Post-Kyoto: Designing the Next
International Climate Change
Protocol**
Matthew Clarke
2008. 978-1-60456-840-0

**Economics of Policy Options to
Address Climate Change**
Gregory N. Bartos
2009. 978-1-60692-116-6

Disputing Global Warming
*Anton Horvath and Boris Molnar
(Editors)*
2009. 978-1-60741-235-9

**The Effects of Climate Change on
Agriculture, Land Resources,
Water Resources, and Biodiversity in
the United States**
*Peter Backlund, Anthony Janetos, and
David Schimel*
2009. 978-1-60456-989-6

**Climate Variability, Modeling Tools
and Agricultural Decision-Making**
Angel Utset (Editor)
2009. 978-1-60692-703-8

**Emissions Trading: Lessons Learned
from the European Union and Kyoto
Protocol Climate Change Programs**
*Ervin Nagy and Gisella Varga
(Editors)*
2009. 978-1-60741-194-9

**Designing Greenhouse Gas
Reduction and Regulatory Systems**
Sonja Enden (Editor)
2009. 978-1-60741-195-6

**Global Climate Change:
International Perspectives and
Responses**
Elias D'Angelo (Editor)
2009. 978-1-60741-233-5

**Constructing Climate Change
Legislation: Background and Issues**
Gerald P. Overhauser (Editor)
2009. 978-1-60692-986-5

Climate Change and its Causes, Effects and Prediction Series

Constructing Climate Change Legislation: Background and Issues

Gerald P. Overhauser
Editor

Nova Science Publishers, Inc.

New York

For permission to use material from this book please contact us:
Telephone 631-231-7269; Fax 631-231-8175
Web Site: http://www.novapublishers.com

NOTICE TO THE READER

The Publisher has taken reasonable care in the preparation of this book, but makes no expressed or implied warranty of any kind and assumes no responsibility for any errors or omissions. No liability is assumed for incidental or consequential damages in connection with or arising out of information contained in this book. The Publisher shall not be liable for any special, consequential, or exemplary damages resulting, in whole or in part, from the readers' use of, or reliance upon, this material.

Independent verification should be sought for any data, advice or recommendations contained in this book. In addition, no responsibility is assumed by the publisher for any injury and/or damage to persons or property arising from any methods, products, instructions, ideas or otherwise contained in this publication.

This publication is designed to provide accurate and authoritative information with regard to the subject matter covered herein. It is sold with the clear understanding that the Publisher is not engaged in rendering legal or any other professional services. If legal or any other expert assistance is required, the services of a competent person should be sought. FROM A DECLARATION OF PARTICIPANTS JOINTLY ADOPTED BY A COMMITTEE OF THE AMERICAN BAR ASSOCIATION AND A COMMITTEE OF PUBLISHERS.

LIBRARY OF CONGRESS CATALOGING-IN-PUBLICATION DATA
Available upon request.

ISBN: 978-1-60692-986-5

Published by Nova Science Publishers, Inc. ✛ *New York*

CONTENTS

PREFACE

Sorting out the appropriate roles of each level of government in addressing climate change is far more complicated than the specific question of whether State climate change programs should be preempted. This book raises more comprehensive and complex questions that the Committee must consider: what roles are best played by each level of government as we marshal our country's resources to address climate change and how should these roles be reflected in Federal legislation. Many State and local governments have begun to address climate change, as the Subcommittee heard last year in testimony from State and local witnesses.2 Activity by State and local governments has helped reduce greenhouse gas emissions, has helped build a consensus that we need to address climate change nationally, and is helping to develop and test different policies.

The country is now at the difficult and familiar stage of transitioning from multiple, often unconnected, State and local climate change programs to a comprehensive, national approach to addressing the global problem of climate change. For a variety of reasons, State and local environmental programs have often led to enactment of Federal environmental legislation.

Chapter 1- The Committee on Energy and Commerce and its Subcommittee on Energy and Air Quality are issuing a series of Climate Change Legislation Design White Papers as the next step in the legislative process leading to enactment of a mandatory, economy-wide climate change program. While the hearings held last year were designed to give the Committee an understanding of the status and projected path of climate change and potential ways to address it, these White Papers and the hearings on them will focus the Committee's attention on crafting climate change legislation. The White Papers and related hearings will lay out basic design and key principles of a program, and also identify issues about which further information and discussion is needed.

This chapter addresses different potential mechanisms for limiting the cost and maximizing the efficiency of a mandatory, comprehensive climate change program to reduce greenhouse gas emissions by 60 to 80 percent by 2050.

Chapter 2- The Committee on Energy and Commerce and its Subcommittee on Energy and Air Quality are issuing a series of Climate Change Legislation Design White Papers as the next step in the legislative process leading to enactment of a mandatory, economy-wide climate change program. While the hearings last year were designed to give the Committee an understanding of the status and projected path of climate change and potential ways to address it, these White Papers and the hearings on them will focus the Committee's attention on crafting mandatory, economy-wide climate change legislation. The White Papers and related hearings will lay out basic design and key principles of a program, and also identify issues about which further information and discussion is needed.

A comprehensive national approach to climate change will be most effective when all levels of government -- Federal, State, Tribal, and local -- play active roles. This chapter is intended to foster discussion of these issues by raising key factors that should be considered in determining what roles are appropriate for each level of government.

Chapter 3- The Committee on Energy and Commerce and its Subcommittee on Energy and Air Quality are issuing a series of Climate Change Legislation Design White Papers as the next step toward enactment of a mandatory, economy-wide climate change program. While the hearings earlier in this Congress were designed to give the Committee an understanding of the status and projected path of climate change and potential ways to address it, these White Papers and the hearings on them will focus on the construction of mandatory, economy-wide climate change legislation. The White Papers will describe the basic design and key principles of a regulatory program and also identify issues about which further information and discussion is desirable.

The first White Paper identified the economic sectors and activities that are directly emitting greenhouse gases (GHGs) and how those emissions could be included in a cap-andtrade program. This chapter discusses potential domestic legislative provisions that could encourage developing countries to curb their emissions of greenhouse gases.

Chapter 4- The Committee on Energy and Commerce and its Subcommittee on Energy and Air Quality are issuing a series of Climate Change Legislation Design White Papers as the next step in the legislative process leading to enactment of a mandatory, economy-wide climate change program. While the hearings earlier in the year were designed to give the Committee an understanding of the status and projected path of climate change and potential ways to address it, these White Papers and the hearings on them will focus the Committee's attention on crafting mandatory, economy-wide climate change legislation. The White Papers will lay out the basic design and key principles of a program, and also identify issues about which further information and discussion is needed.

This chapter addresses the scope and coverage of the climate change program. It discusses what sectors and activities are directly emitting greenhouse gases, and how those emissions could be included in a cap-and-trade program. Other White Papers will address a number of other cap-and-trade design elements and additional topics, including: cap levels and timetables, measures for containing costs in a cap-and-trade program, carbon sequestration, offsets and credits, developing countries, distribution of allowances, and additional measures to complement the cap-and-trade program.

Chapter 5- Since January 2007, the debate over climate change has evolved dramatically, beginning with groundbreaking chapters released by the International Panel on Climate Change, which affirmatively settled the question of whether human activity is contributing to global warming In addition, in the absence of Federal action, some 24 states and several regional organizations have moved towards regulation of greenhouse gases. While the States should be lauded for their progressive stance in addressing the problem, their actions, if not properly coordinated and directed and accompanied by Federal action, could be disruptive to interstate commerce and counterproductive to the goal of limiting national greenhouse gas emissions. Finally, the Supreme Court added another layer of complexity and urgency to our task when it ruled in Massachusetts v. EPA, that CO_2 is a pollutant, with the almost certain consequence that the Environmental Protection Agency (EPA) will in the near term regulate CO_2 emissions under the existing Clean Air Act (CAA), unless Congress enacts a regulatory statute.

In: Constructing Climate Change Legislation...
Editor: Gerald P. Overhauser

ISBN 978-1-60692-986-5
© 2009 Nova Science Publishers, Inc.

Chapter 1

CLIMATE CHANGE LEGISLATION DESIGN WHITE PAPER GETTING THE MOST GREENHOUSE GAS REDUCTIONS FOR OUR MONEY*

Committee on Energy and Commerce

The Committee on Energy and Commerce and its Subcommittee on Energy and Air Quality are issuing a series of Climate Change Legislation Design White Papers as the next step in the legislative process leading to enactment of a mandatory, economy-wide climate change program. While the hearings held last year were designed to give the Committee an understanding of the status and projected path of climate change and potential ways to address it, these White Papers and the hearings on them will focus the Committee's attention on crafting climate change legislation. The White Papers and related hearings will lay out basic design and key principles of a program, and also identify issues about which further information and discussion is needed.[1]

This chapter addresses different potential mechanisms for limiting the cost and maximizing the efficiency of a mandatory, comprehensive climate change program to reduce greenhouse gas emissions by 60 to 80 percent by 2050.

---

*This is an edited, excerpted and augmented edition of a Committee on Energy and Commerce Staff, dated May 2008.

EXECUTIVE SUMMARY

One of the Committee's goals in designing a comprehensive climate change program is to achieve the necessary greenhouse gas reductions for the least cost and with the least economic disruption. Reducing greenhouse gas emissions will be an expensive proposition, but scientists tell us that not reducing emissions will leave future generations with serious problems that will cost even more to address. This chapter discusses ways to keep costs as low as feasible while still achieving our environmental goals.

The most important way to keep costs down is to establish a system that will achieve lowest-cost reductions. The climate change debate often focuses on the need for expensive measures. If the program is structured properly, however, significant reductions can be achieved by economically beneficial measures (i.e. measures with savings that exceed costs). In large part, these measures are improvements in energy efficiency and productivity.

The decision to have a cap-and-trade regulatory program as the cornerstone of a mandatory climate change program is driven in large part by the ability of such a program to reduce greenhouse gas emissions to a specified level at the lowest possible overall cost to society and to lower the cost for regulated entities. As compared to more traditional forms of regulation, a well-designed cap-and-trade program generally should achieve the same environmental results at a lower cost because it provides flexibility to emitters, creates incentives for sources to use low-cost compliance strategies, and provides incentives for technological advances.

While Congress can always pass new legislation modifying the cap-and-trade program if costs are excessive, it may be desirable to provide methods in the initial legislation to respond to cost problems that do not require Congressional intervention. One approach is to establish mechanisms that operate automatically, such as the ability to purchase offset credits and engage in "banking" of emission allowances. Similarly, Congress could authorize, pursuant to predetermined price triggers, a limited amount of system-wide borrowing of allowances. Alternatively, Congress could assign power to a board or agency to determine when system-wide borrowing or other cost containment measures should be initiated.

The cap-and-trade program will include two important features to help reduce costs:

- Regulated entities and other market participants will be able to bank allowances for later use. Allowance banking can help reduce costs by encouraging the use of cost-effective, long-term compliance strategies and by providing a "cushion" to help minimize price fluctuations in the allowance market.

- Regulated entities will also be able to use offsets, provided they are real, verifiable, additional, and permanent. Offsets are measures that reduce greenhouse gas concentrations (such as a forest that sequesters carbon biologically) in a way that would otherwise not be reflected in the cap-and-trade program. Offsets can be less expensive than the marginal cost of reducing emissions covered by the cap and can, therefore, reduce costs and provide flexibility for regulated entities.

The Committee should consider a number of optional features of cap-and-trade programs to help reduce costs.

- The Committee should consider whether to allow each regulated entity to borrow allowances from the future to apply to a current year obligation (firm-level borrowing). It is unclear whether this approach would provide firms with flexibility they would not otherwise have from the allowance market, and it poses some difficult administrative issues (such as how one would determine whether a firm was sufficiently credit-worthy to permit it to borrow allowances).

- The Committee should consider whether to have a compliance period longer than a year. Some believe a longer compliance period could help individual firms reduce costs by allowing them to average out business cycles and unexpected circumstances over a longer time period.

- The Committee should consider whether to provide for a special cost containment mechanism to release additional allowances into the market (i.e., raising the cap for a year) when allowance prices are high for a sustained period. It should also consider whether to make the release self-executing based on a statutory or regulatory formula established at the outset of the program and revised periodically thereafter, or to vest an entity with discretion to release allowances based on certain criteria. Releasing allowances into the market should decrease allowance prices, but could also reduce or delay the environmental benefit of the program, depending on how it is done. This chapter discusses the following four methods of releasing additional allowances, which could be combined or modified in numerous ways:

  o The bill could set a safety valve price and allow the Government to sell an unlimited number of allowances at that price.

- o The cap could be held constant when allowance prices are high and continue to decline when allowance prices drop.
- o A new, independent board could have the authority to borrow allowances from the future and release them in the current year as necessary to prevent significant economic harm.
- o A strategic allowance reserve could be set aside and tapped when allowance prices rise above a certain level.

- The Committee should consider setting a floor for allowance prices as a means for providing minimum price certainty for technology developers.

A number of matters beyond the scope of this chapter will also affect the cost of a comprehensive, mandatory climate change program. They include:

- Additional, complementary measures (beyond the cap-and-trade program) must be reviewed to determine whether they reduce or raise the total cost of achieving the necessary greenhouse gas reductions. Measures such as appliance efficiency standards and local or State energy efficiency programs might achieve economically beneficial or low-cost greenhouse gas reductions that would not be achieved solely through the capand-trade program. Other measures might increase the total cost of reductions by requiring expensive reductions or by adding transaction costs to achieve reductions the cap-and-trade program would achieve on its own.
- The distribution of allowances could affect the cost of the program or the distribution of the cost among regulated entities and other affected parties.
- The interim timetables and targets for greenhouse gas reductions (leading up to the goal of reducing greenhouse gas emissions by 60 to 80 percent by 2050) will also affect the cost of the program.

BACKGROUND

There are two types of costs associated with greenhouse gas reduction programs: the costs of acting and the costs of not acting. This chapter will focus on the costs of acting because one of the Committee's goals is to achieve the necessary greenhouse gas reductions (60 to 80 percent by 2050) for the least cost and while avoiding economic disruption.

In reviewing projected costs of climate change programs, however, it is important to remember that they tell only part of the story; they fail to account for the cost of not acting. For example, an estimate that a climate change program will reduce U.S. Gross Domestic Product (GDP) by 3 percent in 2050 is based on comparing GDP in a world with a climate change program to GDP in a fictional world where there are no controls on greenhouse gases, no climate change, and no measures necessary to adapt to climate change.

To provide context for the discussion of how to contain costs, this section discusses different types of costs associated with reducing greenhouse gas emissions. It first discusses different costs of a comprehensive climate change program. It then briefly describes the costs of failing to reduce greenhouse gases.

Program Costs

When people talk about limiting the cost of the program, they often have different "costs" in mind. In evaluating various methods of limiting cost, it is helpful to be specific about the type of cost one is trying to limit. The "costs" people are trying to affect include:

- the overall, long-term cost to society of reducing greenhouse gases;
- the cost to individual participants of complying with the greenhouse gas reduction program;
- volatility in the price of allowances;
- the average price of allowances over a long (multi-month) time period; and
- the distribution of costs among all entities and people affected by the greenhouse gas reduction program.

Costs can be measured and estimated in a variety of ways, but nearly all approaches involve economic modeling. The Environmental Protection Agency (EPA), the Energy Information Administration, and others use various economic models to analyze and project the effects of different proposed legislative climate change policies, but their results must be reviewed with some degree of caution. The outputs of such models are only projections, based on current knowledge and significantly affected by model assumptions. As such, modeling results are limited in their ability to project future economic effects accurately, especially those costs that will be incurred decades from now. The models are best used to compare differences in policies to see how those differences produce different effects, as well as to identify basic trends and directions.

One commonly used measure of cost for cap-and-trade programs is the allowance price. The allowance price is the marginal cost of reducing an additional ton of carbon dioxide or its equivalent (CO2e), not the average cost of reducing CO2e. If allowance prices are projected to be $20 per ton, theoretically regulated entities should have made all reductions that cost less than $20 per ton. The average cost of reducing emissions to that level would be significantly less than $20 per ton, but the cost of reducing the next ton should be $20. Figure 1 contains EPA's estimates of allowance prices for three different climate change bills, using two different models: S. 280 (McCain-Lieberman), S. 1766 (B ingaman-S pecter), and S. 2191 (Lieberman-Warner). The allowance prices are projected to start in 2015 in the $12 to $15 range for S. 280 and S.

1766, and in the $29 to $40 range for S. 2191. The allowance price for each bill are projected to approximately double by 2030. The higher allowance prices for S. 2191 are driven in large part by the larger required reductions in greenhouse gas emissions, also shown in Figure 1.

Another commonly used measure of cost for a cap-and-trade program is the total cost of abatement. Abatement costs are the net cost of the actions taken to reduce greenhouse gas emissions (e.g., to install and operate carbon capture and storage technology or to improve energy efficiency).[2] EPA's projected total annual costs of abatement for S. 2191, S. 1766, and S. 280, using two different models, are provided in Figure 2 (although EPA notes these are overestimates).

The cost to an individual regulated entity is also an important measure and is often miscalculated. An individual regulated entity's cost is sometimes assumed to be the allowance price multiplied by the number of tons of CO2 that the entity would have emitted if there were no regulation of greenhouse gas emissions. This is likely to be an overestimate of the cost to a regulated entity. First, the regulated entity's cost would be lowered by the number of allowances it receives for free. Second, the regulated entity's cost would be lower if it were to reduce its emissions at a cost less than the allowance price (such as through energy efficiency measures). Third, costs would also be lowered if the entity were able to pass abatement costs on to its customers. In fact, a regulated entity might make money if it were given allowances for free and made sufficient reductions that cost less than the allowance price and/or passed on the cost of allowances to its customers.

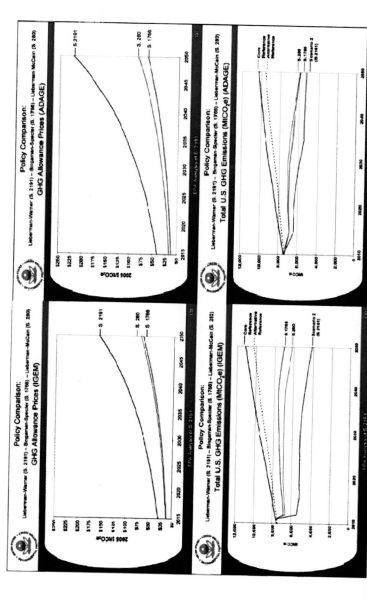

The top two graphs each show projected allowance prices for three Senate bills, and the bottom two graphs show projected total U.S. greenhouse gas emissions for the same bills. The legislated policies modeled in the left-hand graphs are the same as those in the right-hand graphs. The differences between the right- and left-hand projections are due to the use of two different general equilibrium models (IGEM and ADAGE).

Sourse: Environmenlat Protection Agency, "EPA Analysis of the Lieberman – Warner Climate Security Act of 2008," at pp.136-137, 139-140.

Figure 1. Allowance Prices and Emmision Pathways under Legislative Proposals.

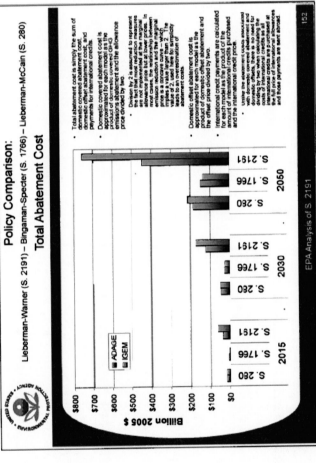

This figure represents estimates from two different models of annual abatement costs in each given year (not cumulative costs) for three different Senate bills. Due to a lack of information, EPA approximated the cost of actions that would be taken to reduce emissions, but did so in a manner that overestimates total abatement costs (as explained in the right-hand column of this slide).

Source: Environmenlat Protection Agency, "EPA Analysis of the Lieberman-Warner Climate Security Act of 2008," at p. 152.

Source: Environmenlat Protection Agency, "EPA Analysis of the Lieberman – Warner Climate Security Act of 2008," at pp.152.

Figure 2. Abatement Costs of Legislative Proposals.

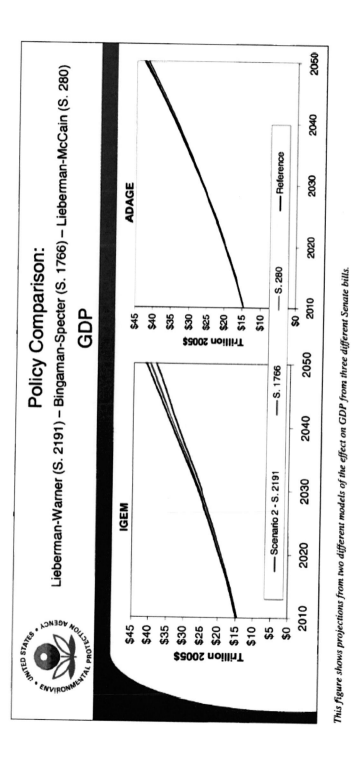

This figure shows projections from two different models of the effect on GDP from three different Senate bills.

Source: Environmenlat Protection Agency, "EPA Analysis of the Lieberman – Warner Climate Security Act of 2008," at pp.10.

Figure 3. Growth of GDP under Legislative Proposals.

Changes in GDP are another measure of the cost to the U.S. of reducing greenhouse gas emissions. EPA's projected changes in GDP for S. 2191, S. 1766, and S. 280, using two different models, are provided in Figure 3.

Other measures of cost include: changes in energy prices (electricity, natural gas, oil, and gasoline), effects on the cost to consumers, effects on different industrial sectors, and the effect on U.S. jobs. This chapter primarily discusses ways to control total costs to society and allowance prices. Measures that control these costs should also help control other types of costs. The distribution of costs among regulated entities and affected parties is generally beyond the scope of this White Paper.

Costs of Inaction

A serious commitment of societal resources to combat climate change is warranted by the damage that is projected to occur if we fail to do our part in global efforts to reduce greenhouse gas emissions. Last year the Intergovernmental Panel on Climate Change projected the following future impacts for the range of climate changes projected over the 21st century:[3]

- Changed ecosystems, including increased risk of extinction for 20-30 percent of the plant and animal species.
- Decreased crop productivity in lower latitudes and, for temperature changes above 5.4 degrees Fahrenheit, decreased crop productivity globally.
- Increased risk to coasts, including coastal erosion, due to climate change and sea level rise.
- Millions more people subject to annual flooding due to sea level rise (by 2080's).
- Potential changes in health status for millions of people due to malnutrition, severe weather events, increased burden of diarrheal disease, changes in infectious disease patterns, and so forth.
- Reduced water availability, reduced hydropower potential, and changing seasonality of meltwater flows from major mountain ranges (where more than one-sixth of the world population lives).
- Decreased water resources in semi-arid areas (including the Western United States).

- Increased flood risk from heavy rainfall events, even in some areas where the mean rainfall is projected to decrease.
- Increased salinisation of groundwater supplies in coastal areas due to sea level rise.

The U.S. will experience some of these climate change effects within our borders, but even those occurring outside our borders could affect us significantly. A chapter by a Military Advisory Board warned that:

> Projected climate change poses a serious threat to America's national security. . . . On the simplest level, [climate change] has the potential to create sustained natural and humanitarian disasters on a scale far beyond those we see today. The consequences will likely foster political instability where societal demands exceed the capacity of governments to cope.[4]

Unfortunately, none of the cost projections of U.S. climate change bills account for the cost we will incur if we do not reduce greenhouse gas emissions. There is a high level of scientific certainty that failing to reduce emissions will cause significant problems, but the methodologies for monetizing the costs of such failure are still in their infancy, owing to the complexity of the subject.

One critical question in attempting to characterize the cost of inaction on climate change is the manner in which a cost estimate should account for the fact that actions taken today will prevent harm that would otherwise occur decades from now.[5] The Stern Review, a comprehensive and controversial review of the economics of climate change done for the British Government, took the view that today's generation should not be able to treat costs it would impose on future generations as less significant than the same costs incurred today. This is the key reason some other economists view as inflated The Review's estimate of the "social cost of carbon" as $85 per ton of CO2e under a business-as-usual scenario (where the world's greenhouse gas emissions remain on their current trajectory).[6] The Review went on to note that this cost of continuing to emit carbon was much higher than the marginal cost of reducing greenhouse gas emissions in many sectors. The same criticism regarding the failure to discount future costs applies to the Review's estimate of net benefits, which are set forth here:

> Comparing the social costs of carbon on a BAU [business as usual] trajectory and on a path towards stabilisation at 550 ppm CO2e, we estimate the excess of benefits over costs, in net present value terms, from implementing strong mitigation policies this year, shifting the world onto the better path

[towards stabilization at 550 ppm]: the net benefits would be of the order of $2.5 trillion. This figure will increase over time. This is not an estimate of net benefits occurring in this year, but a measure of the benefits that could flow from actions taken this year; many of the costs and benefits would be in the medium to long term.[7]

In reviewing estimates of the cost of reducing greenhouse gas emissions, it is important to remember that they look at only half of the story — how much we will spend to reduce emissions. Although we lack agreed-upon analytical methodologies to provide reasonable estimates of the cost of failing to act, those costs should be part of the consideration of what actions to take.

CAPTURING ECONOMICALLY BENEFICIAL AND LOW-COST REDUCTIONS

To limit the overall, long-term cost of reducing greenhouse gas emissions by 60 to 80 percent by 2050, the Committee should establish a system that results in society making the lowest cost reductions (to the extent consistent with other social goals). The measures that a climate change program requires or encourages can have a dramatic effect on the cost of the program. A number of measures create a net economic benefit (e.g., the measure's additional capital cost is more than offset by its lifetime savings). For example, a consumer's electricity bill savings from more efficient lighting can be greater than the extra initial cost of that lighting. Other measures, however, will have a net economic cost. For example, capturing carbon dioxide (CO_2) from electricity generation and sequestering it underground in geologic formations generally does not save money and would not be done absent the need to reduce greenhouse gas emissions (except perhaps in limited circumstances, such as enhancing oil recovery).

It appears that substantial reductions in greenhouse gases could come from measures that would pay for themselves. A recent analysis evaluated hundreds of measures using a bottom-up approach to try to identify the lowest cost greenhouse gas reductions. The resulting report, The McKinsey Report, [8] focused on 250 measures that it determined had a marginal cost of less than $50 per ton and that, when combined, could produce greenhouse gas reductions in 2030 at two different levels of greenhouse gas reductions — one slightly below and one in the range of reductions contemplated by current climate change legislative proposals. The McKinsey Chapter represents an interesting and useful construct for evaluating and analyzing the costs of different climate policies, although its cost estimates should not be taken as definitive.

As illustrated in Figure 4, the chapter found that a significant volume of greenhouse gas reductions can occur in a manner which provides a net economic benefit to the United States.[9] For a 3.0 gigaton CO_2e reduction in 2030 (from projected annual emissions of 9.7 gigatons), the chapter concluded that "Almost 40 percent of abatement could be achieved at 'negative' marginal costs, meaning that investing in these options would generate positive economic returns over their lifecycle."[10]

A few notes about this analysis are warranted. First, the "net" cost estimates do not account for the economic benefit of reducing greenhouse gas emissions or other air pollutants. These measures are projected to be economically beneficial on their own. Second, the analysis was largely concluded before enactment of the Energy Independence and Security Act of 2007 (EISA). Therefore, some of the opportunities for efficiency improvements may overlap with requirements in EISA. For example, the significant strengthening of the vehicle fuel efficiency standards in EISA is not reflected in The McKinsey Chapter's baseline. Finally, there is no universal agreement on the cost estimates presented in The McKinsey Chapter.[11] The Committee should use those cost estimates as illustrative, rather than definitive.

Economically beneficial reductions may seem too good to be true. One would think that people and companies would already be implementing measures that have a net economic benefit. Some early movers are doing so. For example, a rural Indiana school district reduced its energy usage by 38 percent and saved $1.77 million in energy costs over 43 months (meeting its 7-year rate of return goal in 3 1/2 years),[12] The country's biggest private consumer of electricity, Wal-Mart, recently recognized substantial improvements in its bottom line by reducing CO_2 emissions through wide-ranging energy efficiency improvements. The company's accounting of its carbon dioxide emissions revealed cost-saving energy efficiency opportunities such as retrofitting refrigerator cases (reducing more than 15,000 metric tons CO_2 and saving $2.6 million annually) and installing auxiliary power units in trucks (reducing 100,000 metric tons CO_2 and saving $25 million annually),[13]

There are many reasons why companies, governments, and consumers have not taken advantage of economically beneficial measures to reduce greenhouse gas emissions. For example, the person who purchases a good may not be the one who pays for its electricity use, so the extra cost would be borne by one person and the savings reaped by another. This would be the case where a landlord buys the refrigerator and the tenant pays the electricity bill. Also, people may not have sufficient information to make the economically rational choice.

Consumers may underestimate the annual and lifetime costs from inefficient appliances such as refrigerators. They retain old ones when energy cost savings would justify replacement with a new one, and they choose less costly but less efficient models when energy cost savings would justify buying more expensive, efficient models.

It is not just individual consumers that fail to take advantage of economically beneficial greenhouse gas reduction opportunities. Companies that have voluntarily reduced emissions have found that the mere requirement to track and monitor their CO2 emissions (or energy usage) has led to ways of reducing those emissions (or energy usage) that save money.[14]

We cannot meet our greenhouse gas reduction goals solely by reliance on measures with a net economic benefit. Maximizing the use of such measures to the extent consistent with other goals, however, will help offset the cost of other measures, thereby reducing the net cost of a greenhouse gas program. We need to design a comprehensive climate change program that will encourage or require greenhouse gas reduction measures with a net economic benefit or low economic cost.

CAP-AND-TRADE REGULATORY PROGRAM — CORNERSTONE OF A LOW COST PROGRAM

The decision to have a cap-and-trade regulatory program as the cornerstone of a mandatory climate change program is driven in large part by the ability of cap-and-trade to reduce greenhouse gas emissions to a specified level at a lower overall cost, and with greater flexibility for regulated entities, as compared with traditional command-and-control regulation.[15] Relative to more traditional forms of regulation, a well-designed cap-and-trade program should achieve the same environmental results at a lower cost because it provides flexibility to emitters, creates incentives for sources to use low-cost compliance strategies, and rewards technological advances.

In a cap-and-trade regulatory program, the Government establishes the maximum level of emissions allowed in each year (i.e., it caps emissions), and distributes allowances (by allocation formula or auction) equal to that level. (This chapter will assume that one allowance authorizes the emission of one ton of CO2 (or its equivalent).)

Figure 4 – Abatement Measures with Estimated Costs and Contributions

U.S. MID-RANGE ABATEMENT CURVE – 2030

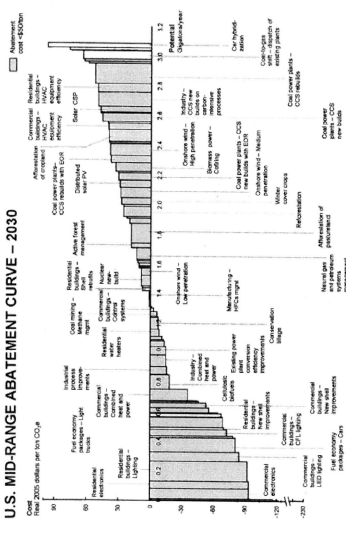

This figure shows projected cost per ton of CO_2e (vertical axis) and greenhouse gas reduction potential (horizontal axis) for a variety of measures.

Source: McKinsey and Company, "Reducing U.S. Greenhouse Gas Emission: How much ar What Cost? (Dec. 2007) at p.viii.

Figure 4. Abatement measures with estimatedCosts and Contributions.

Regulated entities (and others) can then buy and sell allowances. At the end of the compliance period, the regulated entities must turn in to the government allowances in an amount equal to the emissions for which they have responsibility under the program.

A cap-and-trade program with broad coverage can also help make the climate change program fairer. It would help ensure that all sectors in the economy do their fair share in addressing climate change. By incorporating the price of carbon into the price of goods and services, the cap-and-trade program helps ensure that people who are causing carbon emissions bear more of the cost of those emissions. Currently, the price of goods with large carbon footprints does not reflect the true cost of the good to society because the price does not reflect the damage from climate change.

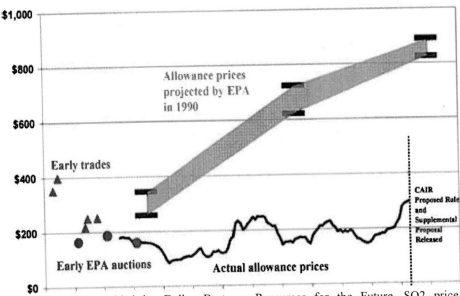

Source: Graph provided by Dallas Burtraw, Resources for the Future. SO2 price projections taken from the Environmental Protection Agency, Comparison of the Economic Impacts of the Acid Rain Provisions of the Senate Bill (S.1630) and the House Bill (S.1630), (July 1990). Actual price trajectory and early market data taken from Ellerman et al., Markets for Clean Air: The U.S. Acid Rain Program, (2000). CAIR is the Clean Air Interstate Rule, which revised the use of Acid Rain SO2 Allowances and thus disrupted the displayed trend line.

Figure 5. Actual Costs of Acid Rain Program Lower than Projected Costs SO2 Allowance Prices (2005$/ton).

The Acid Rain cap-and-trade program, established in the Clean Air Act Amendments of 1990, is generally regarded as both an environmentally and economically successful program. It has significantly reduced sulfur dioxide emissions and the resulting damage caused by acid rain at a cost far less than was estimated when it was adopted in 1990. See Figure 5. The cost of the reductions has also been estimated to be less than the cost of achieving the same reductions through traditional source-specific performance standards. See Figure 6. The flexibility as to when, how, and where reductions occurred played a significant role in the lower costs. A greenhouse gas cap-and-trade regulatory program will be far more complicated than the Acid Rain Trading Program, but the same basic principles leading to low-cost reductions should apply.

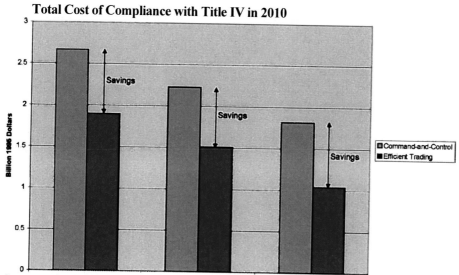

Source: Figure generated with data from Carlson et al., "Sulfur Dioxide Control by Electric Utilities: What are the Gains from Trade?" Journal of Political Economy, (2000), Table 2, at p. 1313.

Figure 6. Estimated Savings from Acid Rain Trading Program Compared to Traditional Command-and-Control Approach.

Flexibility

A cap-and-trade regulatory program puts the choice of compliance strategies in the hands of the private sector, rather than the Government. It is based on the assumption that the private sector is better than the Government at selecting low-cost compliance options. Different entities facing different circumstances can tailor compliance programs on an on-going basis in a way that the Government would never have the resources, flexibility, or information to allow in a traditional regulatory program. Entities can react to changing information and circumstances by adjusting compliance strategies without obtaining approval from the Government.

In contrast, using traditional regulatory approaches as the cornerstone of a comprehensive climate change program could pose a number of downsides and is less likely to result in the lowest cost reductions.[16] Under a traditional regulatory approach, the Government would set performance standards, emission rates and/or technology requirements to determine what actions all regulated entities must take. It would be very difficult for the Government to take into account the different circumstances faced by each of the regulated entities. Providing flexibility to industry by tailoring decisions to each entity (as would happen in a permitting or waiverprocess) would be quite resource-intensive for both the Government and the regulated entity. On the other hand, selecting a standard applicable to many entities could disproportionately burden some sources and/or not achieve all the cost-effective reductions. In addition, the Government is unlikely to have all the accurate information necessary to require the lowest cost reductions, especially given that costs will change over time.

The Acid Rain Trading Program provides a good example of how this flexibility could be used. Regulated power plants were given allowances. Each plant could then do any of the following:

- Reduce its emissions to equal the allowances it had been given.
- Over-control its emissions and sell the extra allowances to another plant or save them for later use.
- Or under-control its emissions and buy extra allowances from another plant (or use allowances that it banked in a year that it over-controlled).

Electricity generators were allowed to select their own emission reduction strategies. They could increase the efficiency of their plants, switch to low sulfur coal, install pollution control equipment (scrubbers), encourage their consumers to use electricity more efficiently so that the power plant did not need to burn as much coal, switch to a fuel source (e.g., renewable, natural gas, or nuclear) that does not emit sulfur dioxide, or any combination of those actions. Companies could also pick different compliance strategies for different plants, allowing them to phase in pollution control installations over a number of years as it made economic sense for them to do so.

Incentives for Low-Cost Reductions

Under a cap-and-trade regulatory approach, the reductions that are cheapest should be made first. For example, if Company A can reduce emissions for $5 per ton and allowances are selling for $20 per ton, it will have an incentive to reduce emissions even if it were given enough free allowances to cover all of its emissions. This is because Company A can sell its allowances to others for more than the cost of reducing its own emissions. If it costs Company B $100 per ton to make reductions when allowances are selling for $20 per ton, it will have an incentive to continue emitting and acquire enough allowances to cover its emissions. Under this scenario, Company B could cover its emissions by buying 1,000 allowances from Company A. Company B would save $80,000 by buying allowances instead of reducing its emissions, and Company A would have a net profit on the sale of $15,000.

One difference between the Acid Rain Trading Program and the climate change cap-andtrade regulatory program is that the point of regulation (i.e., the entity that has to turn in allowances to the Government) in the climate change program will not always be the entity that actually emits the greenhouse gases.[17] Despite this difference, the program should still provide incentives for emitters to select low-cost methods of reducing emissions. For example, in the transportation sector, fuel providers, rather than emitters (vehicle owners), may be the point of regulation. Fuel providers presumably would incorporate the price of allowances into the cost of fuel. The higher fuel price should provide vehicle owners/emitters with the same economic incentive to reduce their emissions as if they were required to turn in allowances themselves. For example, a delivery company with a large fleet of vehicles would presumably have the same incentive to reduce CO_2 emissions (by using more efficient vehicles or improving driving patterns) whether it paid for its emissions through a fuel surcharge or had to turn in allowances directly.

Theoretically, a cap-and-trade regulatory program (regardless of point of regulation) will generally incorporate the price of carbon into goods and then allow the people in the stream of commerce to select compliance strategies by reacting to that price.[18] There are instances, however, when the allowance cost will not be fully passed along. For instance, if a company has significant competition from companies or products not subject to the same regulation, it may not pass along the full cost of the allowances.

Incentives for Technology Advances

Cap-and-trade also rewards and, thereby, encourages technology development and innovation, which should help lower the cost of the program compared to a more traditional regulatory program with the same level of environmental protection. Caps that become more stringent over time provide a financial incentive to develop technology that will achieve greater emission reductions at a lower cost. Because a cap allows technology to be phased in over time (instead of requiring all sources to install a new technology within a short time period), it facilitates continuous improvement of the technology; later users can make adaptations based on the experience of early movers.

A cap-and-trade program also reduces the risk associated with using new technology to reduce emissions. Using a new control technology to meet traditional regulatory programs carries some risk that it will not work as well as expected (possibly resulting in a source being out of compliance with the law), and no chance of reward if it works better than expected. In contrast, in a cap-and-trade program, if new technology underperforms, a source can cover the deficit by purchasing more allowances. If a new technology overperforms, it directly benefits the source's bottom line by reducing the number of allowances a source needs.

Principles for Smart Program Design and Implementation

In designing a cap-and-trade program, the Committee will keep in mind the following principles, which can help keep costs down:

- Certainty: Certainty in program rules helps regulated entities and other affected parties make efficient compliance decisions. Long-term certainty is important because compliance requires long-term capital investment.
- Sufficient Lead Time: Regulated entities and other affected parties need sufficient lead time before the program starts to assess compliance options and construct necessary capital equipment. Sufficient lead time also helps avoid early run-ups in allowance prices.
- Market Liquidity: The Government's failure to release allowances to the market in a timely manner will increase prices. Whatever allowance distribution methodologies the Government uses, allowances should be distributed and available to the market prior to the end of the compliance period.[19]

- Good Information: The market needs to know actual emissions, both before the program starts and periodically during the compliance year.[20] Participants need to understand what is happening in the market. Under the Acid Rain Trading Program, allowance ownership is public information. In addition, trade magazines and brokers provide price information.

- Simplicity: Simple, clear rules help regulated entities understand their compliance obligations and can help reduce the cost of a program in the long run. Although a special rule for a unique circumstance may seem reasonable on its own, a multitude of special rules taken together can make a program so complicated that it takes experts and lawsuits to determine the rules. As one witness told the Subcommittee, "If..the devil is in the details, then the more details there are, the more places there are for the devil to hide."[21]

Market Mechanisms to Manage Risk

Under a cap-and-trade regulatory program, the private sector will be able to develop a range of methods to help individual firms manage and control their own compliance costs. In a healthy market for carbon allowances, the allowance price will go up and down in response to underlying changes in market fundamentals. Although this volatility is one sign of a healthy market, it raises the concern that fluctuating allowance prices will unnecessarily increase costs for regulated entities. That concern has led some to question how the Government could design the program to protect regulated entities from excessive allowance price fluctuations. Although the Government can include certain design elements in the program (e.g., allowing unlimited banking), a cap-and-trade regulatory program does not need to rely solely on the Government to manage all contingencies. The private sector will also play an important role in helping businesses manage risk and minimize the cost effects from price fluctuations.[22]

In existing cap-and-trade regulatory programs for sulfur dioxide and nitrogen oxide, the private sector currently uses financial instruments to enable companies to manage the cost of complying with these programs. In particular, futures, forwards, and options allow a company to lock in a future supply of allowances at a price that is known today — smoothing costs over time. Undoubtedly, these and similar tools will be developed and used for the carbon market to help cushion businesses from unexpected changes in allowance prices and to provide some certainty about future compliance costs.

OPTIONAL CAP-AND-TRADE PROGRAM FEATURES TO CONTROL COSTS

There are a number of program features that can be added to a basic cap-and-trade program to enhance the program's ability to avoid unnecessarily high costs. Two of these, banking and the use of offsets, will be included in the cap-and-trade program. The Committee should also consider using additional cost containment measures.

Banking

The cap-and-trade program will allow unlimited banking of allowances.[23] Banking allowances should help reduce the overall, long-term cost of making necessary emission reductions, lessen cost to regulated entities, and reduce volatility in the allowance market. A basic cap-and-trade program provides flexibility as to who emits where. Banking enhances the advantages of a cap-and-trade program by providing flexibility as to when emissions occur, and does so without undermining the environmental goals of the program. While the same overall emission reductions are obtained with or without banking, banking encourages firms to make some reductions earlier than they normally would; in essence trading their lower-cost early reductions for higher-cost later reductions. Reducing greenhouse gas emissions earlier than required by the cap will not decrease the environmental benefit of the program.

In some cap-and-trade programs, allowances can be used for the specific compliance period for which they are issued or for any later compliance period (although each allowance may only be used once). For example, in the Acid Rain Trading Program, companies could use allowances issued for 1995 in that year, or they could save or "bank" them to cover emissions in 1996 or any later year. In this Program, companies over-controlled in the early years and banked a significant number of allowances. See Figure 7.

In contrast, in some cap-and-trade programs, allowances from one compliance period cannot be used in a later compliance period. For example, in Phase 1 of the EU ETS, allowances could only be used during the first phase of the program (2005-07), and could not be used for later years.

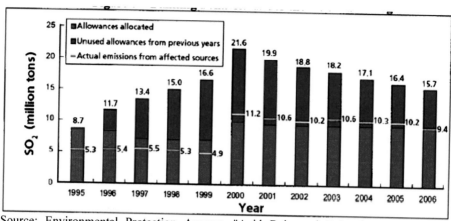

Source: Environmental Protection Agency, "Acid Rain and Related Programs 2006 Progress Report," (2007), at p. 9, accessed 5/5/08 at http://www.epa.gov/ airmarkets /progress/docs/2006-ARP-Report.pdf.

Figure 7. Banking Behavior under the Acid Rain Program.

Banking can help reduce costs by encouraging companies to adopt compliance strategies that are more cost-effective over the long-term, instead of focusing solely on short-term compliance. Sources that over-control in the early years by installing control technology before it is needed can offset part of the cost by saving extra allowances for later sale or use. In contrast, the lack of banking in Southern California's Regional Clean Air Incentives Market (RECLAIM) program is believed to have discouraged firms from adopting long-term compliance strategies. [24]

Banking can help protect against short-term volatility (ups and downs) in allowance prices by providing a "cushion" both on a firm-level and a system-wide basis. On a firm-level basis, for example, an industrial plant might want to over-control in the early years (by making the plant more efficient) and "bank" its extra allowances so that it can use them in case of an unexpected increase in its emissions (due perhaps to equipment malfunction or a sudden upswing in business). If a large number of market participants bank allowances, a similar cushion is created to protect against systemic circumstances which cause higher emissions than expected. For example, when economic growth is slow, emissions might decrease, which should result in banking of allowances. Those banked allowances will then be available for sale or use when economic growth picks up.

Offsets and International Trading

A full discussion of offsets and international trading, including their advantages and disadvantages, is beyond the scope of this chapter and will be addressed in a subsequent White Paper. Nonetheless, it is important to note that they provide an opportunity for reducing the cost of the cap-and-trade program and for reducing allowance prices.

The cap-and-trade program will allow the use of offsets, although the extent to which they can be used is beyond the scope of this chapter. To ensure the environmental integrity of the cap, offsets must be real, additional, verifiable and permanent. There are people seeking to limit offsets, but any limit on offsets could effectively limit the incentives to develop technologies that would produce offsets.

Offsets allow regulated entities to meet their obligation to turn in allowances by using credits generated by reducing or sequestering greenhouse gas emissions outside of the cap. For example, sources of greenhouse gas emissions cannot be covered by the cap if they are not measurable. Methane leaking from landfills, for example, cannot be measured easily, and largely for that reason, landfills emitting methane will not be regulated entities under the cap-and-trade program. If, however, methane from landfills is captured and converted into energy, the decrease in greenhouse gas emissions can be measured. A landfill owner could install equipment to capture methane and convert it into energy and create "offsets" that could be sold to a regulated entity and used like an allowance to cover the regulated entity's emissions (provided that the owner's actions were not otherwise required by law).

The Committee will also need to address whether to link the U.S. cap-and-trade program to international trading programs, and the extent to which the program should allow the use of international credits or offsets. Factors to consider include the effect on cost and on developing countries' incentives to limit greenhouse gas emissions.

Allowing regulated entities to use offsets can reduce the cost of allowances and the cost of a cap-and-trade program because many offset opportunities are projected to cost less than the marginal cost of reducing emissions from covered sources. For example, EPA compared the projected allowance prices for S. 2191 using several different assumptions about the ability to use domestic and international offsets. See Figure 8. S. 2191 limits both the use of domestic offsets and the use of international credits to 15 percent each of the total allowances that must be turned in each year. EPA projected that, if instead the bill were to allow unlimited use of domestic offsets and international credits, it would reduce allowance prices by about 70 percent. In contrast, EPA projected that, if S. 2191 were changed to preclude the use of any domestic offsets or international credits, it would increase allowance prices by more than 90 percent.

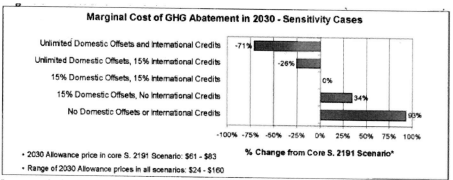

In general, the tighter the limit on the amount of domestic or international offsets that can be used, the higher the projected price path of allowances.

Source: Environmental Protection Agency, "Offsets and Climate Policy: EPA Perspectives," (March 26, 2008) at p. 7. Accessed 05/12/08 at http://carbonoffsetproviders.org/7.html.

Firm-Level Borrowing from the Future

The Committee should consider whether an individual firm should be able to borrow allowances from the future.[25] This would permit a regulated entity to meet a current-year compliance obligation with future-year allowances. For example, an entity would be able to turn in 2018 vintage allowances to cover its 2015 emissions.

Firm-level borrowing is often mentioned as a way of reducing the cost to individual regulated entities. A firm might want to borrow from the future for several years until it installs new control technology that will dramatically reduce its emissions; installing the technology sooner might not be economically or technologically feasible. A firm might also want to borrow from the future if it were to miscalculate and have insufficient current allowances to cover its current emissions.

Firm-level borrowing from the future on a small-scale or a short timeframe is unlikely to change the environmental outcomes of a cap-and-trade program. Nonetheless, firm-level borrowing from the future does pose environmental or economic risks and potentially significant administrative issues.

Perhaps the biggest concern expressed about firm-level borrowing from the future is that firms will borrow a significant number of future allowances and then default. Depending on how the borrowing is structured, a default could cause environmental harm by resulting in more emissions than allowed by the program (because the borrowed allowances are never paid back). Another scenario that has been raised is that companies would engage in excessive borrowing, creating such significant liabilities that Congress would feel compelled to step in and bail the companies out by relieving them of their obligation to reduce emissions. This would have adverse environmental consequences, penalize companies that had met their obligations, and might even create a degree of uncertainty sufficient to cause significant instability in the allowance market. Alternatively, defaulting firms could increase the cost of the program for others by decreasing the number (and thus increasing the price) of allowances that should have been available in the years from which they were borrowed.

Firm-level borrowing from the future could also pose administrative issues. For example, consider a firm that borrows future-year allowances from a Government "bank." Presumably, the firm would have to pass some type of credit-worthiness test, put up some type of collateral for the borrowed allowances, and then agree to pay back the allowances over time with interest. Finn-level borrowing might be simpler if a firm could take future-year allowances that it owns and use them for current year compliance.[26] In either type of borrowing, though, the system would have to be carefully designed to prevent profiteering on borrowed allowances, to guard against defaults, and to minimize the economic and environmental consequences of defaults.

Given the administrative burdens and potential for defaults, it is important to focus on the problem that firm-level borrowing from the future is meant to address and determine whether it is really desirable or whether there is a better way to address the problem. If the allowance market is functioning well, a firm that needs extra allowances for a few years until it installs new technology or because it miscalculated its allowance needs should be able to purchase current-year allowances in the market, use allowances that it has banked, or trade future-year allowances that it owns for current-year allowances. If those options were not available (or economical) because the market is not functioning well (i.e., if allowances prices were unexpectedly high for a sustained time period), then regulated entities might find firm-level borrowing particularly useful. If there is a systemic problem, however, system-wide, rather than firm-level, borrowing might be a more efficient solution. In system-wide borrowing, future allowances are made widely available to regulated entities to cover current emissions. One way to accomplish systemwide borrowing would be to have the Government take allowances from a future year and release them into the market for current use.

Questions:

If the allowance market is functioning well, what problems would finn-level borrowing from the future solve?

If the allowance market is not functioning well, would system-wide borrowing be a better solution than finn-level borrowing?

If firm-level borrowing from the future were allowed:

- What mechanisms should be used to protect against defaults?
- Should borrowers have to pay interest? In dollars or allowances? How should the interest be set?
- Should a borrower have to prove credit-worthiness? How?
- What type of collateral (if any) should be required to borrow allowances?
- How far into the future could allowances be borrowed?
- How quickly should allowances have to be paid back?
- What limit, if any, should there be on how many allowances a firm could borrow?
- What system-wide limit, if any, should there be on the total amount of allowances that could be borrowed from or in a specific year? If there should be a limit, should borrowed allowances be available on a first-come first-served basis? Should there be another means of apportioning them?
- Should anyone be allowed to borrow from the future? Or only regulated entities?
- Would firm-level borrowing create opportunities for market manipulation? If so, would there be ways to protect against that?

Multi-Year Compliance Periods

The Committee should consider the appropriate length of the compliance periods (i.e., how frequently allowances must be turned in to cover emissions). Different trading programs have different compliance periods.[27] The minimum length of the compliance period should be one year, but it might be appropriate to have a longer compliance period, which might reduce the cost to regulated entities and reduce volatility in the market.

A two- or three-year compliance period would provide regulated entities more flexibility than a one-year compliance period. Instead of issuing allowances for a specific year, allowances could be issued for the full compliance period and used to cover any emissions during that compliance period. This method might help contain the cost of a climate change program by reducing volatility in the allowance market and allowing regulated entities to average their emissions over a longer time period. Effectively, it is a way of allowing a limited amount of system-wide borrowing with minimal administrative burden.

A multi-year compliance period might raise concerns that regulated entities might not pay sufficient attention to their allowance needs and face a shortage at the end of the period. A longer compliance period would not, therefore, change the requirement that regulated entities report actual emissions periodically during the year. Annual, interim obligations to turn in allowances might also be appropriate.

A variation on a multi-year compliance period would be to permit regulated entities to use allowances one year in advance of the year for which they are issued. For example, to cover emissions in 2012, regulated entities could turn in allowances from 2012 or 2013; to cover emissions in 2013, regulated entities could turn in allowances from 2012, 2013, or 2014. To decrease the potential for abuse or default, regulated entities could be limited to meeting no more than a specified percent of their obligation in any given year with allowances from the following year. Effectively, this would allow regulated entities to "borrow" some allowances one year in advance with minimal administrative burden.

Questions:

- How long should the compliance period be?
- What are the potential downsides of a multi-year compliance period and how could they be minimized?
- Would a multi-year compliance period help reduce cost either system-wide or for individual regulated entities?
- If a multi-year compliance period were adopted, should regulated entities be required to turn in allowances annually?
- Alternatively, should regulated entities be permitted to use allowances one year in advance of the year for which the allowance is issued? If so, should there be a limit on how many future allowances a regulated entity can use at a time?

SPECIAL COST CONTAINMENT MECHANISMS: SAFETY VALVE, CIRCUIT BREAKER, INDEPENDENT AGENCY, AND STRATEGIC RESERVE

The Committee should consider the use of one of a variety of special cost containment mechanisms that would release additional allowances into the market to reduce costs. Releasing additional allowances into the market essentially raises the cap for that year (allowing more emissions), which should have the effect of lowering allowance prices, and thus lowering the cost of complying with the program.

In determining the viability of each of these mechanisms, a critical question is how it would affect the environmental integrity of the cap-and-trade program. The answer would depend in part on whether the additional allowances would increase cumulative emissions through 2050. Cumulative emissions should not increase if allowances were to be taken from one year and moved into a different year (such as would happen if allowances were borrowed from the future).[28] In contrast, if new allowances were created, then cumulative emissions might increase. The effect on the environmental integrity of the program would also depend on how many allowances could be added in a given year.

The best way to design a mechanism to release additional allowances will depend, to a certain extent, on the cost "problem" the Committee is trying to address. The following are the two primary competing potential goals of mechanisms for releasing additional allowances:

- To lower the cost of the program (by lowering allowance prices) in the event that unexpected or unusual circumstances lead to unexpectedly high allowance prices over a sustained period (such as six months or longer); or
- To cap costs instead of emissions by providing certainty about the maximum cost per allowance.[29]

The first goal would guard against a dramatic rise in allowance prices due to unusual and unexpected circumstances. Rather than relying on creative legal interpretations by regulatory agencies in the event of unexpectedly high allowance prices, it might be better to design flexibility into the program to handle unusual circumstances. In effect, Congress would be deciding that, if costs were in the range of what is projected, emission reductions must be achieved on the timetable set out in the statute. Only if something unexpected were to happen should the timetable and reduction targets be adjusted.

The second goal represents a very different approach. In effect, Congress would be deciding the maximum amount to spend on reducing greenhouse gas emissions regardless of the level of reductions it would achieve.

If the first goal were adopted (to protect against unexpectedly high allowance prices), and allowance prices were projected to range from $25 to $35 per ton, then Congress might direct that the cap be raised slightly (or temporarily) when allowance prices hit $60 or more per ton. If the second goal were adopted (to provide certainty about the maximum cost), Congress might direct that the cap be loosened when allowance prices hit $20. That would reflect a decision by Congress that, no matter what the scientists tell us about the dangers of climate change, Congress is only willing to require reductions that cost $20 or less per ton.

Another potential goal deserves special discussion. One motivation for mechanisms to release additional allowances into the market is the desire to ensure that someone (other than Congress) will have the authority to "fix" a long-term problem with the program for fear that Congress will not intervene even if the program is creating significant harm to the U.S. economy over many years. While it is certainly wise to design a system that has some ability to adapt to changing or unforeseen circumstances, it is unrealistic to believe that Congress will not address climate change again for 40 years, especially if there are major problems with the program.

Special cost containment mechanisms for climate change cap-and-trade programs have evolved over the last few years. There are more potential mechanisms to release additional allowances into the market than can be discussed in this chapter, and each mechanism has numerous potential modifications. The trigger price for releasing allowances is key to all of these approaches. Rather than providing an exhaustive discussion of all the options, this chapter will provide a flavor of the options being discussed by focusing on four different mechanisms:

- a safety valve and unlimited allowances;
- a circuit breaker that holds the cap constant when allowance prices are unexpectedly high;
- an independent agency with the broad discretion to release additional allowances; and
- a strategic allowance reserve and an agency with limited discretion to release additional allowances.

For each of these, the description below is a broad overview of how that type of mechanism might work. The methods could be combined or modified in a number of ways.

Safety Valve And Unlimited Allowances

In 2005, Senator Bingaman issued a discussion draft of a climate change cap-and-trade program that included a "safety valve" as a way of containing costs.[30] Under that legislative draft, regulated entities could meet their compliance obligation either by turning in allowances or by making a "safety valve" payment of $7 per ton of CO2e emitted in 2012 (with the payment increasing at a rate of 5 percent each year).[31] In S. 1766, Senators Bingaman and Specter modified this concept, increasing the payment to $12 per ton of CO2e emitted in 2012. The payment would increase at a rate of 5 percent each year above inflation, bringing it to $25 per ton CO2e in 2030.[32] They also renamed the safety valve payment a "Technology Accelerator Payment" (TAP). Essentially, the safety valve or TAP releases an unlimited number of additional allowances into the market at the price specified in the legislation.

The result of this safety valve or TAP would be that, instead of capping the amount of emissions each year, the program would cap the cost of emissions per ton. Figure 9 shows that, starting in 2020, the projected cumulative emissions with a TAP (area under the gredn line) would exceed the cumulative emissions allowed by the cap operating without a TAP (area under the red line).[33] This is because the safety valve price (red dotted line in Figure 10) was set lower than the projected price of allowances in the same program without a TAP (green and blue lines). Instead of reducing emissions to a level at or below the cap, regulated entities were projected to comply with these requirements through a combination of reducing some emissions and making safety valve payments.

The Bingaman-Specter safety valve would help contain costs by creating certainty about the maximum cost per ton of CO2e. It would also be relatively easy to implement because Congress, as part of the final legislation, would make the hard decisions about what allowance price would trigger the safety valve and how many allowances would be released.

The primary concern that has been raised with the Bingaman-Specter safety valve is that it is projected to prevent the program from achieving the necessary greenhouse gas reductions and environmental goals. This is because the safety valve price was set lower than the projected allowance price.

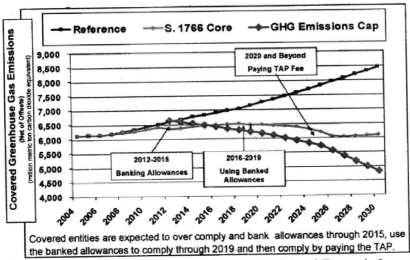

Source: Energy Information Administration, "Energy Market and Economic Impacts of S.1766, the Low Carbon Economy Act of 2007," (January 2008), at p. 8, accessed 5/5/08 at http.11www.eia.doe.gov/oiaifservicerpt/lcea/pdf/sroiaf(2007)06.pdf.

Figure 9. Effect of Safety Valve on Emissions Pathway.

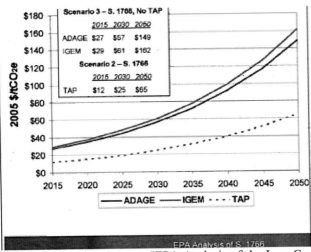

Source: Environmental Protection Agency, "EPA Analysis of the Low Carbon Economy Act of 2007; 5.1766 in the 110th Congress," (January 15, 2008), at p. 31, accessed 5/5/08 at http://www.epa.gov/ climatechange/economics/ pdfs/S1766_ EPA_ Analysis.pdf.

Figure 10. Safety Valve Trigger Price Compared with Expected Allowance Prices.

Another major problem that has been raised is that the safety valve price would likely decrease the incentive to develop and deploy new technology. Pollution control technology may be less expensive than initially expected. With a safety valve near or below the projected allowance price, potential technology may be dropped due to a mistaken early estimate that the cost will exceed the safety valve price. Also, some firms might prefer the certainty of safety valve payments and fail to invest in technology that might cost less in the long run, but is riskier. Finally, it would be difficult for Congress to decide now on the right safety valve price each year for the next 40 years.

An important consideration in using a safety valve is the level at which it is set. A safety valve set below the expected marginal cost (or allowance price) would be much more likely to be triggered, which would result in emissions above the cap. If the safety valve were set significantly higher than the marginal price, it would be less likely to be triggered. A high safety valve would be less likely to result in emissions above the cap, but would do less to ensure that the cost of the program is not greater than anticipated.

A safety valve coupled with making unlimited allowances available at the safety valve price is particularly well-suited to achieving the second goal discussed above — providing absolute price certainty regardless of the level of reductions achieved. If one wanted only to protect against unexpectedly high allowance prices, the safety valve price could be set well above the projected range of allowance prices.

A "circuit breaker" approach is an alternative method of releasing additional allowances into the market. During time periods when the average annual allowance price exceeded a predetermined "circuit breaker" price, the cap would be held constant, rather than continuing to decline. If the average allowance price for a year were to drop below the circuit breaker price, then the cap would continue declining at its initial rate. Figure 11 illustrates a situation where the circuit breaker is in effect for a few years and then, when allowances prices decline, the cap continues its previous rate of descent. S. 309 (Sanders-Boxer) includes a circuit breaker, which it calls a "technology-indexed stop price."[34]

Inclusion of a circuit breaker would help address one of the difficulties with establishing a cap for greenhouse gas emissions — uncertainties about when technology will be developed and deployed. For example, when EPA projects allowance prices for particular cap-and-trade programs, it makes assumptions about the pace at which new nuclear capacity could be deployed. If those assumptions turn out to be too optimistic, the cost of meeting a declining cap could be much higher than anticipated.

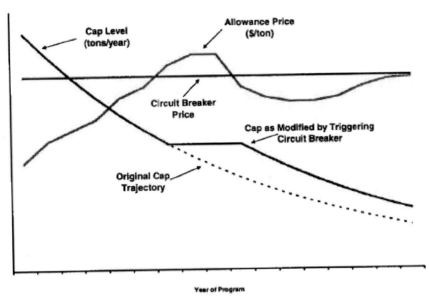

Source: Figure provided by Energy and Environment Associates.

Figure 11. Theoretical Operation of a Circuit Breaker Mechanism.

A circuit breaker would hold the cap constant until new nuclear capacity (or some other technology) comes on line and brings the allowance price down. While the cap is being held constant, there would continue to be an incentive to develop and deploy new technology because allowance prices would be above the circuit breaker price.

This approach provides less certainty about price than a safety valve with unlimited allowances because the allowance price may still rise after the circuit breaker is triggered. It provides more certainty about environmental benefits because there is still a cap (although it may be larger than the cap initially set in the statute). If, however, the circuit breaker were triggered, cumulative emissions over the length of the program would be greater than without the circuit breaker.

This approach would help meet the first goal, protecting against unexpectedly high prices due to unforeseen circumstances. It would not meet the second goal of providing price certainty because prices could rise above the price that would trip the circuit breaker.

This approach would require Congress or an agency to make difficult decisions about the price at which to set the circuit breaker and whether (and how) the price trigger should change over time.

Independent Agency with Broad Discretion to Release Allowances

The debate on special cost containment mechanisms was changed dramatically with the introduction of S. 1874, which was later modified and incorporated into S. 2191 as reported out of the U.S. Senate Committee on Environment and Public Works on December 5, 2007 (Sections 2601-05). Rather than the statute setting a safety valve price and allowing essentially an unlimited number of additional allowances into the market, the bill would establish a new, independent government board (the Carbon Market Efficiency Board or Board), modeled after the Federal Reserve Board of Governors. The bill would delegate to the Board the authority to decide the timing and number of any additional allowances to be released into the market by borrowing them from the future, based on a determination of what was necessary to prevent significant harm to the U.S. economy.[35]

The Board would have authority to implement different sets of "cost relief measures" as necessary to prevent significant economic harm. Most importantly, the Board would be able to borrow allowances from future years (by reducing the caps in those years) and release those allowances to the market. The Board would also be able to increase the number of allowances that regulated entities could borrow from their future allowances, lengthen the payback period of loans to regulated entities, or lower the interest rate on loans. (This group of measures would only be useful in a system that allows firm-level borrowing.) In addition, under S. 2191, the Board would be able to increase the quantity of offsets or foreign allowances that could be used.[36]

The bill would provide the Board very broad discretion regarding the use of these cost relief measures.[37] The Board may carry out measures "to ensure a functioning, stable, and efficient market," but "only as needed to avoid significant economic harm" and only for one year at a time.[38] The Board would have to ensure that borrowed allowances would be paid back in 15 years. Otherwise, the Board would have broad discretion. The amount of allowances that could be released, when they could be released, and the year from which the allowances could be borrowed are among the decisions that would be left to the discretion of the Board and its determination of what is needed to avoid significant economic harm. The bill would not require the Board to issue rules to establish guidelines for how it would exercise its discretion or to provide an opportunity for public comment or participation. Nor does the bill provide for judicial review of the Board's decisions. [39] The Board was designed to operate independently of political influence. It would be comprised of 7 members with staggered 14-year terms[40]The members would be Presidential appointees requiring Senate confirmation, and could not hold other employment during their terms of service. The members could be removed by the President for cause.

Several benefits of this approach have been noted. It could protect against significant unexpected economic harm, and do so in a way that does not increase cumulative greenhouse gas emissions over the life of the program.[41] It also would avoid the difficulty of having Congress decide on a specific safety valve price or how many allowances could be released each year for the next 40 years.

A number of concerns have been raised about this approach. For one, it would add uncertainty to the cap-and-trade program. Regulated entities would not know when the Board would make additional allowances available, which would make it difficult to predict future allowance prices. This uncertainty could hinder investment in the development of new technologies. The Federal Reserve, for example, took many years to evolve to the point of relative predictability that it exhibits now. Also, starting a new agency from scratch poses logistical and practical problems that may seem mundane, but that would take considerable energy and time to solve.

More importantly, though, this approach raises a fundamental question about what decisions should be made by elected, politically accountable representatives of the American people, and what decisions should be delegated to expert agencies with little accountability. The question arises from both the nature of the decisions left to the Board and the limited checks on its actions.

The decisions delegated to the Board are significant from both environmental and economical perspectives. (For example, the Board could decide to double the level of emissions allowed in any given year, or it might decide that an average allowance price of $150 a ton in 2015 is acceptable.) Essentially, the Board would have the ability to weaken the timetables and targets adopted by Congress. The bill would give the Board significant discretion — with the main limit being the Board's determination of what is necessary to prevent significant economic harm.

Broad grants of discretion on significant environmental and economic decisions are not uncommon, but the decisions are usually subject to a greater level of political and judicial accountability than this approach would provide. The Board is designed to operate free of political influence, which may have advantages, but also means that neither the President nor the Congress would have much control over it. [42] Some perceive this political independence as beneficial because they fear that a politically accountable Board might interfere in the market or decrease the environmental benefits of the program to meet short-term political needs. (For example, a Board that served at the pleasure of the President might be pressured into releasing additional allowances into the market to reduce allowance prices (and therefore gasoline prices) right before an election, or might refuse to release allowances even if the allowance price were very high.) This approach relies on substantial faith in the ability of the President and the Senate to ensure that the right people are selected as Board Members. In addition, it seems unlikely that the Board could be held to account in the Courts if it deviated from Congressional intent. The need for the Board's actions to be quickly implemented to react to the allowance market would seem to make judicial review impractical (even if the bill provided for it).

Ironically, Congress would create this new Board with almost unfettered discretion in the hope that, were the cap-and-trade program to work as Congress intends, this Board would have nothing to do other than to collect information and prepare reports,[43] because the Board's main function would be to intervene if the program were not working. This could make it difficult to attract and retain members with the appropriate skills, wisdom, and experience to make the decisions entrusted to it. Alternatively, if the Board were to attract highly qualified members, they might try to enlarge its mission to make the Board relevant and interesting.

It is unclear whether this Board would better meet the first goal (protecting against unexpectedly high allowance prices) or the second goal (limiting the price of allowances regardless of the environmental consequences). It would depend, at least in part, on how the Board interpreted its charge to "prevent significant harm to the U.S. economy." It does appear, however, that the Board is designed to meet the goal of ensuring that someone can "fix" the program if something goes wrong and Congress does not meet its responsibility to step in.

STRATEGIC ALLOWANCE RESERVE AND AN AGENCY WITH LIMITED DISCRETION TO INTERVENE IN THE MARKET

An alternative cost containment mechanism would be to create a strategic allowance reserve by setting aside a fixed percentage of each year's allowances from the start of the program through 2050.[44] If allowance prices were too high for a sustained period, the implementing agency would auction some of the reserve allowances. No more than a fixed percentage (perhaps 5 or 10 percent) of the initial reserve could be released in any calendar year. If prices were within expected bounds in the early years, the reserve would serve as system-wide banking of allowances for use in later years. If prices were higher than expected in the early years, releasing the allowances would function as system-wide borrowing of allowances from the future.[45]

Under this alternative, the climate change legislation would provide the implementing agency with limited discretion in using the reserve. For the first part of the program (perhaps the first 10 years), Congress would provide specifics such as: the average allowance price that would trigger the release of allowances; the time period over which the average allowance price would be measured (perhaps six months); the number of allowances that would be released; and the timing and method of release. For example, the legislation might require that, if average allowance prices were too high for two quarters in a row, then in the next quarter the implementing agency would be required to sell one-fourth of the reserve allowances that could be released in that year.

Although the rules governing release of reserve allowances for the first part of the program would be set in legislation, Congress could require the implementing agency to issue rules (subject to judicial review) governing release of reserve allowances for subsequent periods of time (perhaps every 10 years).[46] At a minimum, these rules would have to set the allowance price that would trigger the release of allowances. The bill might also give the agency limited discretion to change other factors (such as when and how the allowances are released) as necessary to improve the efficient functioning of the market.

This approach would require Congress to make some very hard decisions in the climate bill, such as how high is too high for an allowance price. If the purpose of the strategic reserve is to protect against unexpected high prices to prevent significant economic harm, then the dollar value that would trigger a release of reserve allowances would need to be set significantly above projected allowance prices for each year and be adjusted for inflation. Setting it too close to the projected allowance price would be likely to interfere with the market and decrease the incentives for industry to develop and deploy breakthrough technologies. Congress would also have to set forth criteria that would sufficiently limit the implementing agency's discretion for the rules to be issued governing the later periods of the program. Setting these criteria in a way that provides meaningful direction to the implementing agency and reviewing courts might not be easy.

Agency decisions made by rulemaking could be challenged in court. Because the rules for releasing allowances would either be set by Congress or through rulemaking by the implementing agency, political interference with the actual release of the allowances would be difficult. The head of the agency would be appointed by the President and confirmed by the Senate, and would serve at the pleasure of the President.

This approach is designed to meet the first goal. It is based on the assumption that the cap-and-trade market needs some built-in flexibility to protect against significant economic harm if the market does not quite work as projected in the short or medium run (e.g., unusual circumstances lead to high allowance prices for a year, or deployment of carbon capture and storage technology takes a couple of years longer than expected). It also recognizes that, if there is a serious, long-term flaw (e.g., carbon storage technology does not work), Congress has the responsibility to step in. Congress would have ample warning and time to craft solutions before it would need to act; by limiting the allowances that could be released in any given year, it would take a decade or longer of sustained high prices before the reserve would run dry.

Variations

The discussion in this section provides just a flavor of the range of special cost containment mechanisms available to release additional allowances into the market if the Committee were to decide that was an appropriate tool to help contain costs. The options discussed above could be modified or combined in many different ways.[47]

The mechanisms outlined above could also be used to introduce additional flexibility into the market in other ways. Before additional allowances are released into the market, a lower trigger price might raise the limit (if there is one) on the number of offsets that could be used or might change the terms of firm-level borrowing from the future (if that were allowed).

Questions:

- Should a cap-and-trade program have a mechanism for releasing additional allowances into the market to protect against sustained, unexpectedly high allowances prices?
  - Are there reasons other than sustained, unexpectedly high allowance prices for releasing additional allowances into the market?
- What factors should be used to set the average allowance price that would trigger the release of additional allowances into the market?
  - How should the trigger price compare to the projected allowance price?
  - How long do allowance prices need to be high?
- Should the trigger price be set by the Congress in statute or by an agency or board?

- Should the allowances be extra ones that add to cumulative emissions? Or should they come from another year (either borrowed from future years or banked from past years), and thus not increase cumulative emissions?
- Should there be a limit on the number of allowances that could be released in any given year?
  - If so, should that limit be set by Congress or by an agency or board?
  - If Congress should set it, what should the limit be? What factors should Congress consider in setting it?
  - If an agency or board should set it, what, if any, constraints should there be on the discretion of the agency or board?
- Should there be a limit on the total number of allowances that could be released during the life of the program (such as by setting up a reserve)?
  - If so, should that limit be set by Congress or by an agency or board?
  - If Congress should set it, what should the limit be? What factors should Congress consider in setting it?
  - If an agency or board should set it, what, if any, constraints should there be on the discretion of the agency or board?
- How should the allowances be released?
  - According to that year's allocations? Auctioned? First-come first-serve? Fixed price?
  - To whom should they be released? Regulated entities only? Everyone?
- How do the different allowance release mechanisms affect the incentives to invest and innovate?
- Should other types of flexibility be allowed when lower allowance price triggers are hit, such as allowing greater use of offsets?
  - If so, what flexibility should be allowed and at what trigger price?
  - Should it be set in statute? Or left to an implementing agency?
- Should authority to release additional allowances be delegated to an existing agency or agencies? Which one (s)? Or should a new agency be created?
- Does the implementing agency need to be independent? If so, to whom should it be accountable and in what way?
- To what extent should the implementing agency's decisions be judicially reviewable?

- To what extent do any of these potential mechanisms introduce opportunities for players in the market to manipulate it? Are there methods to limit the potential for manipulation?

A Price Floor for Allowances

Although concern centers on excessively high allowance prices, allowance prices that are too low could also be problematic. Low allowance prices (or the potential for them) may fail to encourage investment in new, low-carbon technologies that will be necessary for large-scale emission reductions in later years. Low allowance prices might also be an indication that we can afford to lower the emissions cap.

The Committee should consider whether a floor for allowance prices should be set, and determine whether it should be done via legislation or delegated to a board or agency. One approach would be to give authority to the implementing agency to buy allowances in the market when prices are low. Allowances obtained by the implementing agency could be placed into a reserve for later release during a period of excessively high allowance prices.

Questions:
- Should there be a price floor for allowances?
- Should the implementing agency be authorized to buy allowances in the market when prices drop below the price floor?
- What should the price floor be?
  - Who should set it?
  - What factors should be considered in setting it?
  - What should happen to the allowances obtained or kept as a result of the price floor? Should they be retired? Or saved for later release in the event that prices are too high?

Complementary Measures

Although generally beyond the scope of this White Paper, complementary measures can affect the cost of a comprehensive climate change program. As other measures are proposed, the Committee should carefully review whether they are likely to increase or decrease the total cost of reducing greenhouse gas emissions. Figure 12 illustrates how complementary measures can affect allowance prices and the total cost of reducing greenhouse gases. Congress adopted a number of complementary measures when it passed EISA last year, including more stringent fuel efficiency standards for motor vehicles and a number of measures to improve efficiency of buildings, industry, appliances, and lighting. Complementary measures might include regulations establishing greater energy efficiency in appliances, funding for research and development of new technologies, and performance standards for certain industrial facilities.

Some measures may help reduce cost by requiring economically beneficial or low-cost reductions that the market is likely to miss. In a perfect market, a cap-and-trade program that puts a price on carbon should result in the greatest reductions at the lowest costs (represented by Column A in Figure 12). The market, however, is not perfect, and people do not always respond in the most economically rational way. For example, even though lower operational costs would more than offset the higher initial cost of a more efficient water heater, a consumer might not have enough information to determine that the more expensive water heater would be cheaper in the long run, might not be planning to stay in the house long enough to recoup the higher initial costs, or might not have sufficient resources to cover the higher initial cost at the time of purchase. As a result of these imperfections in the market, a cap-and-trade program is likely to miss some of the low-cost reductions, as represented by Column B in Figure 12.

Some measures may help reduce long-term costs by requiring or encouraging technology development that a cap-and-trade program might not encourage on its own early on, particularly with respect to long-lasting equipment. For example, costs tend to decline as new technologies are commercialized and used on a wide scale. For some technologies, it may be appropriate to subsidize or otherwise encourage their development and deployment though the pilot- and early-commercial phases, in order to accelerate their introduction into widespread commercial use. Doing so might entail designing regulations or incentives to achieve reductions that cost more than the then-current allowance prices (as represented by Column D in Figure 12). (For example, Sections 3601-3605 of S. 2191 (as passed out of Committee) award "bonus" allowances for early deployment of carbon capture and storage at electricity generation plants.) The total cost of reductions could temporarily increase as a result, but benefits would accrue once large-scale, cost-effective reductions from that technology became feasible.

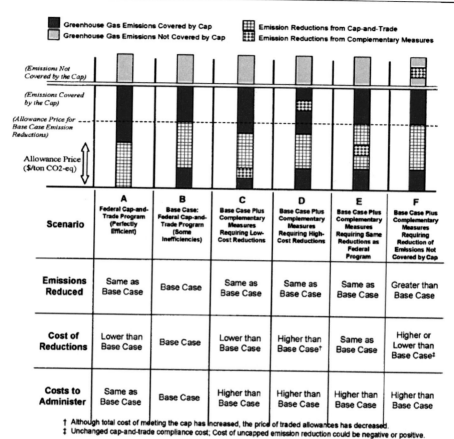

Scenario	A Federal Cap-and-Trade Program (Perfectly Efficient)	B Base Case: Federal Cap-and-Trade Program (Some Inefficiencies)	C Base Case Plus Complementary Measures Requiring Low-Cost Reductions	D Base Case Plus Complementary Measures Requiring High-Cost Reductions	E Base Case Plus Complementary Measures Requiring Same Reductions as Federal Program	F Base Case Plus Complementary Measures Requiring Reduction of Emissions Not Covered by Cap
Emissions Reduced	Same as Base Case	Base Case	Same as Base Case	Same as Base Case	Same as Base Case	Greater than Base Case
Cost of Reductions	Lower than Base Case	Base Case	Lower than Base Case	Higher than Base Case†	Same as Base Case	Higher or Lower than Base Case‡
Costs to Administer	Same as Base Case	Base Case	Higher than Base Case	Higher than Base Case	Higher than Base Case	Higher than Base Case

† Although total cost of meeting the cap has increased, the price of traded allowances has decreased.
‡ Unchanged cap-and-trade compliance cost; Cost of uncapped emission reduction could be negative or positive.

Abatement cost impacts of the complementary policies are independent of the implementing authority (i.e. whether at the local, state, or federal level).

Figure 12. Effects of Complementary Policies on Cap-and-Trade Abatement Costs.

Some measures may, however, increase the cost of reducing emissions. For example, a regulation might require specific types of control technology to be installed at industrial facilities that would have likely been installed anyway to meet the cap. If this were to happen, there would be no environmental benefit and there would be additional transaction costs in setting, meeting, and enforcing the control technology regulation. (See Column E in Figure 12.) Similarly, a regulation of facilities whose emissions are covered by the cap might require specific types of control technology that have a cost per ton greater than the allowance price. In this case, the high-cost reductions would be made instead of lower cost reductions (as represented by Column D in Figure 12). The allowance price would go down, but the total cost of reducing greenhouse gas emissions would go up.

DISTRIBUTION OF ALLOWANCES OR PROCEEDS FROM THE SALE OF ALLOWANCES

The distribution of allowances (or proceeds from the sale of allowances) can affect the total cost of the program, as well as the distribution of costs among regulated entities and other persons affected by the cap-and-trade program. Although an in-depth discussion of this issue is beyond the scope of this White Paper, the following are some ways in which the distribution of allowances could affect cost:

- Allowances targeted to accelerate research, development, or deployment of new technologies could reduce the overall cost of the program.
- Allowances targeted to speed deployment of carbon capture and storage from coal- fired power plants could help deter fuel switching to natural gas, which could help address potential economic disruption from high or volatile natural gas prices.
- Allowance revenues distributed to consumers in a way that prevents them from feeling the price of carbon could make the program more costly overall by not giving individuals incentives to reduce energy consumption. (If, on the other hand, consumers still "felt" the price of carbon in energy prices, but were compensated with allowance revenues in a way that did not mask that price, the incentive to reduce energy consumption would be retained.)
- Allowances dedicated to programs designed to overcome market barriers to the low (or no) cost carbon reductions (such as energy efficiency improvements) could reduce the overall cost of the program.

BIG AND SMALL PLAYERS IN THE SAME MARKET

The cost to individual firms is affected by their ability to develop and implement a cost- effective compliance strategy. An economy-wide cap-and-trade program will require both small and large regulated entities to participate in an allowance market that will also be open to sophisticated financial institutions.

Different regulated entities will have different levels of sophistication and trading experience. For example, the electricity sector has a great deal of experience with pollution allowances due to the Acid Rain Trading Program and should have the skills to adapt to a carbon trading program with relative ease. For other sectors, however, a trading program will require rethinking their methods of complying with environmental regulation and the acquisition of trading skills they may not have now. A smaller industrial company run by engineers, which currently does not employ traders, might not have a large enough financial stake in the carbon market to justify paying close attention to a carbon allowance market. Undoubtedly private firms will develop services to help smaller firms manage their emissions and allowances. The Committee is interested in whether there are ways to design the cap-and-trade program that would assist smaller, less sophisticated firms in complying in a cost-effective manner.

Questions:

- What types of regulated entities are likely to be smaller players in the allowance market?
- Will private sector firms develop services to assist smaller firms develop and implement cost-effective strategies to comply with the cap-and-trade program?
- Are there ways to design the cap-and-trade program to help smaller firms develop and implement cost-effective strategies to comply with the cap-and-trade program?

CONCLUSION

The Committee has a number of options for designing a comprehensive climate change program to achieve the goal of reducing greenhouse gas emissions by 60 to 80 percent by 2050 while keeping costs as low as is feasible.

REFERENCES

[1]   The White Papers are available at http://energycommerce.house.gov /Climate_Change/index.shtml

[2]   Note that abatement costs should be significantly less than the required reductions multiplied by the allowance price.

[3]   Intergovernmental Panel on Climate Change (IPCC), Climate Change 2007: Synthesis Report. Contribution of Working Groups I, II and III to the Fourth Assessment Report of the Intergovernmental Panel on Climate Change [Core Writing Team, Pachauri, R.K and Reisinger, A. (eds.)] (2007) at pp. 48-49.

[4]   The CNA Corporation, National Security and the Threat of Climate Change, (April 2007) at p. 6. The Military Board was comprised of "a dozen of the nation's most respected retired admirals and generals." The report also states that "Climate change acts as a threat multiplier for instability in some of the most volatile regions of the world..Economic and environmental conditions in already fragile areas will further erode as food production declines, diseases increase, clean water becomes increasingly scarce, and large populations move in search of resources. Weakened and failing governments, with an already thin margin for survival, foster the conditions for internal conflicts, extremism, and movement toward increased authoritarianism and radical ideologies."

[5]   Sir Nicholas Stern, The Economics of Climate Change: The Stern Review (January 2007) at pp. 31-32. Usually economic analyses use a discount rate that values goods today more highly than the same type of goods years from now (basically for the same reasons that many of us would prefer to have $100 today rather than $1,000 several decades from now). It is unclear, however, that discounting is appropriate when a later generation will bear the cost for actions taken (or not taken) by our generation.

[6]   /bid at pp. xvi-xvii.

[7]   Ibid at p. xvii.

[8]   McKinsey & Company, Reducing U.S. Greenhouse Gas Emissions: How Much at What Cost? (Dec. 2007). The analysis assumes that the price of oil varies between $50 and $69 per barrel from 2005 to 2030. Ibid at p. 78. Higher oil prices should reduce the cost of some options and/or make more options available at a cost less than $50 per ton CO_2e.

[9]   The report concluded that "The United States could reduce greenhouse gas emissions in 2030 by 3.0 to 4.5 gigatons of CO_2e using tested approaches and high-potential emerging technologies. These reductions would involve pursuing a wide array of abatement options available at marginal costs less than $50 per ton, with the average net cost to the economy being far lower if the nation can capture sizable gains in energy efficiency." Ibid at p. ix (footnote omitted). The report notes that annual U.S. greenhouse gas

emissions "are projected to rise from 7.2 gigatons CO2e in 2005 to 9.7 gigatons in 2030." Ibid at p. x.

[10] Ibid at p. xii. The report gave 3.5 to 5.2 gigatons as the abatement implied by proposed legislation and concludedthat 4.5 gigatons could be achieved at a marginal cost less than $50 per ton CO2e, but did not state an estimate of how much of the 4.5 gigatons could be achieved with options that have a net economic benefit. Ibid at p. x.

[11] For example, many in the auto industry do not believe that there are fuel economy packages for cars and light trucks at the cost estimated by The McKinsey Report that do not change the consumer's utilization of the vehicle.

[12] The Evening Star, "DeKalb Central Saves $2 Million: District Conserves Energy to Save Programs, Staff, Library Funding" (Jan. 16, 2005); The Evening Star, "DeKalb Central Cuts Its Energy Use by 38 Percent" (April 21, 2008).

[13] Wal-Mart Stores, Inc. "Sustainability Progress to Date 2007-2008," (November 15, 2007) at p. 42, http://walmartfacts.com/reports/2006/ sustainability/documents/SustainabilityProgressToDate2007-2008.pdf (accessed 3/25/08).

[14] Companies that have voluntarily joined EPA's Climate Leaders program with greenhouse gas emissions reduction goals have subsequently recognized considerable financial improvements related to emissions control. For example, SC Johnson calculated a 20 percent rate of return on one strategy adopted to meet its Climate Leaders goal, which the company then expanded further to obtain additional cost savings. EPA, A Program Guide for Climate Leaders; Setting the Standard for Greenhouse Gas Management (March 2007) at p. 5, accessed 5/5/08 at http://www.epa.gov/stateply/documents/cl_programguide_508.pdf.

[15] A cap-and-trade program is an appropriate regulatory tool to accomplish the environmental goals of addressing climate change because the geographic location of greenhouse gas emissions does not affect the environmental consequences. In contrast, under traditional air pollution, people closest to the source are often affected more than people farther away from the source.

[16] As discussed in a later section in this chapter, traditional regulatory approaches for some types of reductions may, however, be necessary to complement a cap-and-trade program. For example, appliance efficiency standards may be appropriate to overcome market barriers that would otherwise limit the ability to achieve economically beneficial reductions.

[17] See the first White Paper (Oct. 3, 2007) for a discussion of point of regulation in a cap-and-trade program.

[18] Pizer, Billy "Scope and Point of Regulation for Pricing Policies to Reduce Fossil-Fuel CO2 Emissions," Assessing U.S. Climate Policy Options (Nov. 2007) at p. 73.

[19] For example, if allowances are provided to States, the allowances for 2012 should not be distributed at the end of 2012.

[20] The lack of knowledge of actual emissions was one of the major causes of several problems in the EU ETS, including the over allocation of allowances initially and the large drop in prices when the actual emissions data was released after the program started. Ellerman, Denny and Buchner, Barbara, Over-Allocation or Abatement? A Preliminary Analysis of the EU-ETS Based on 2005 Emissions Data," MIT Center for Energy and Environmental Policy Research, (November 2006), p. 5, accessed 5/5/08 at http://web.mit.edu/ceepr/www/publications/workingpapers/2006-016.pdf.

[21] Written Testimony of Dallas Burtraw, March 29, 2007, Hearing, Subcommittee on Energy and Air Quality, Committee on Energy and Commerce.

[22] Ai outn gh the private sector can help manage risk, there are also concerns that the private sector can unnecessarily increase risk or cost. Some have expressed concern, for example, about market manipulation or that speculation in allowance markets by non-regulated firms will make it difficult for regulated entities to obtain sufficient allowances at reasonable prices to cover their obligations. The Committee is interested in suggestions for methods of reducing the risk of speculation and manipulation in the allowance market.

[23] To verify and authenticate allowances, the implementing agency may need to limit the time period for which an allowance can be banked.

[24] Environmental Protection Agency, Tools of the Trade: A Guide to Designing and Operating a Cap-and-Trade Program for Pollution Control (June 2003) at p. 3-20.

[25] Borrowing from the future must be distinguished from borrowing currently-issued allowances from other private entities, which would be allowed by the program. For example, in 2015, Party A could loan 2015 vintage allowances to Party B under whatever terms were amenable to the two parties.

[26] A firm could own future-year allowances either because the Government has allocated the allowances to the firm or because the firm bought them.

[27] The Acid Rain Trading Program requires all regulated entities to turn in allowances once a year to cover the last year's emissions. The Regional Greenhouse Gas Initiative (RGGI) in the Northeast generally uses a 3-year compliance period that would be extended to 4 years under certain circumstances.

[28] If a significant number of allowances are moved from the future to cover current emissions, it could create unachievable caps in the later years. If this were to happen, Congress might be compelled to increase the cap in the later years.

[29] Releasing additional allowances into the market generally is not considered to be a good way of addressing short- term fluctuations in the market, even if prices are unexpectedly high for a short time period.

[30] The draft bill was named the "Climate and Economy Insurance Act of 2005," but was not formally introduced.

[31] Sections 1512(13) and 1516 of the Climate and Economy Insurance Act of 2005.

[32] Environmental Protection Agency, EPA Analysis of the Low Carbon Economy Act of 2007 (January 15, 2008) at p. 33. Dollar amounts given in 2005 dollars.

[33] This effect was more pronounced when the safety valve was set at $7 per ton.

[34] See Section 2 of S. 309, adding Section 704(f)(2)(D)(ii) to the Clean Air Act.

[35] The Board would also be responsible for collecting and analyzing allowance market information.

[36] The intent is that the Board would consider the use of the other cost relief measures before borrowing allowances from the future.

[37] For simplicity, this paper only discusses the Board's authority after the first two years. Sec. 4(d)(2) and 5(a)(3) of S. 1874, which provide authority for cost control measures in the first two years of the program, are far more prescriptive.

[38] Although Sec. 3(a) of S. 1874 states that one purpose of the Board is to "promote the achievement of the environmental objectives of the United States," the language governing the use of cost relief measures does not specifically require the Board to take environmental considerations into account. It is somewhat unclear how Sec. 4(d), which says that the Board "shall carry out such cost relief measures" if the Board determines that the allowance market "poses a significant harm to the economy of the United States," interacts with Sec. 5(a)(1), which allows the Board to carry out cost

relief measures "to ensure functioning, stable, and efficient [allowance] markets," but only to the extent "needed to prevent significant economic harm during the applicable allocation year."

[39] Sec. 5(a)(2) of S. 1874 would require the Board to "specify the terms of the [cost] relief to be achieved" and to submit to Congress "a report describing the actions carried out by the Board and recommendations for the terms under which the cost relief measure should be authorized by Congress and carried out by Federal entities."

[40] Terms of initial members would be shorter than 14 years to the extent necessary to have one member's term expire every 2 years.

[41] Although the bill would not allow the Board to increase cumulative emissions, excessive borrowing from future years could cause such unrealistically low caps in future years that Congress would be forced to increase those caps (and thus increase cumulative emissions). Shifting a significant amount of emissions from future to current years could also have detrimental environmental effects by delaying greenhouse gas reductions.

[42] Although the President can remove a Board Member, he can do so only for cause. Congress could also enact new legislation overriding the Board or changing its mandate.

[43] It is unclear why a new Board would need to collect information, analyze the program, and prepare reports. Presumably these functions could be served by the agency running the program and/or by agencies charged with market oversight

[44] If there were a price floor for allowances, allowances obtained by the implementing agency could be added to the reserve.

[45] If the implementing agency were to obtain allowances due to a price floor, they could be added to the strategic reserve. This would increase the amount of banking from years in which allowance prices are much lower than expected.

[46] In case the agency rule were delayed or overturned in court, the statute would need to have a back-up provision to protect against market disruptions.

[47] The special cost containment mechanisms being discussed in the Senate include variations on the mechanisms discussed above.

In: Constructing Climate Change Legislation... ISBN 978-1-60692-986-5
Editor: Gerald P. Overhauser © 2009 Nova Science Publishers, Inc.

Chapter 2

CLIMATE CHANGE LEGISLATION DESIGN WHITE PAPER APPROPRIATE ROLES FOR DIFFERENT LEVELS OF GOVERNMENT*

Committee on Energy and Commerce

The Committee on Energy and Commerce and its Subcommittee on Energy and Air Quality are issuing a series of Climate Change Legislation Design White Papers as the next step in the legislative process leading to enactment of a mandatory, economy-wide climate change program. While the hearings last year were designed to give the Committee an understanding of the status and projected path of climate change and potential ways to address it, these chapters and the hearings on them will focus the Committee's attention on crafting mandatory, economy-wide climate change legislation. The chapters and related hearings will lay out basic design and key principles of a program, and also identify issues about which further information and discussion is needed.

A comprehensive national approach to climate change will be most effective when all levels of government -- Federal, State, Tribal, and local -- play active roles. This paper is intended to foster discussion of these issues by raising key factors that should be considered in determining what roles are appropriate for each level of government.[1]

---

* This is an edited, excerpted and augmented edition of a Committee on Energy and Commerce Staff, dated February 2008.

EXECUTIVE SUMMARY

Sorting out the appropriate roles of each level of government in addressing climate change is far more complicated than the specific question of whether State climate change programs should be preempted. This Paper raises more comprehensive and complex questions that the Committee must consider: what roles are best played by each level of government as we marshal our country's resources to address climate change and how should these roles be reflected in Federal legislation.

Many State and local governments have begun to address climate change, as the Subcommittee heard last year in testimony from State and local witnesses.[2] Activity by State and local governments has helped reduce greenhouse gas emissions, has helped build a consensus that we need to address climate change nationally, and is helping to develop and test different policies.

The country is now at the difficult and familiar stage of transitioning from multiple, often unconnected, State and local climate change programs to a comprehensive, national approach to addressing the global problem of climate change. For a variety of reasons, State and local environmental programs have often led to enactment of Federal environmental legislation.

Industry is often interested in Federal legislation to avoid or replace a patchwork of State regulations, which helps reduce the burden on companies involved in interstate commerce. Federal environmental standards create a level environmental playing field among States (i.e., Federal legislation will ensure that all citizens in all States can enjoy a basic level of public health and environmental protection without fear of driving industry and jobs to States with lower environmental standards). Another major reason for Federal environmental programs is to address situations where pollution released in one State causes environmental or public health problems in another State. Federal programs can also provide resources for environmental protection where State and local programs are insufficient.

This national approach will need to include a variety of programs at each level of government. A quick look at differing governmental roles in existing programs illustrates that it is typical for a given program to have separate and distinct roles for Federal, State, Tribal, and/or local governments. For example, in one of the most federally-oriented air pollution control programs, the Acid Rain Trading Program, State and local governments have the authority to inspect power plants to determine whether they are in compliance with monitoring requirements. On the other hand, economic development and land use decisions are typically left to local, Tribal, and State governments, but the Federal Government may provide grants or other incentives to encourage smart growth development.

Addressing climate change will require employing a variety of tools. The primary tool at the Federal level will be a national, economy-wide cap-and-trade program that reduces greenhouse gas emissions by 60 to 80 percent by 2050. Other tools that could be used include appliance efficiency standards, building codes, land use decisions, performance standards, public transit, and incentives to increase efficiency. Some tools will be more effective and appropriate in the hands of State, Tribal, or local governments; others will work better in Federal hands.

A comprehensive, national approach to climate change will require a melding of different governmental roles and tools. Given the breadth of actions that will be necessary to reduce greenhouse gas emissions and to adapt to climate change, Federal, State, Tribal, and local governments will need to play a variety of roles.

This chapter is intended to explore the key factors that the Committee will need to consider and balance as it constructs a national greenhouse gas control program and seeks to rationalize the roles of different levels of government. These factors include:

- the global effect of greenhouse gas emissions;
- the effect on the level and cost of national greenhouse gas reductions;
- the efficient use of government and societal resources;
- the benefit of States, Tribes, and localities as laboratories;
- differing local circumstances;
- the burden on interstate commerce;
- imposition of costs on other States; and
- stakeholder needs.

BACKGROUND

State and Local Climate Change Programs

In 2006, California became the first State in the nation to establish an economy-wide cap on its greenhouse gas emissions by enacting AB 32, the Global Warming Solutions Act.[3] This requires California to reduce its greenhouse gas emissions to 25 percent of 1990 levels by 2020 and 80 percent by 2050 through a combination of regulations and market mechanisms.

Sixteen States have since adopted overarching greenhouse gas emission reduction targets (six of them codified).[4] Nearly 800 mayors in communities representing more than 77 million Americans from all 50 States have signed the U.S. Conference of Mayors Climate Protection Agreement, whereby they agree to reduce community-wide greenhouse gas emissions by 2012 to at least 7 percent below 1990 levels.[5] A report last year found that many cities will not be able to meet this goal absent complementary State and Federal policies to reduce greenhouse gas emissions.[6] In mid-2007, a multi-state Climate Registry was launched to establish a common protocol for greenhouse gas emissions reporting due to the lack of such a protocol at the Federal level. The Registry now has 39 member States plus the District of Columbia.[7] See Figure 1.

States are entering into regional partnerships to address climate change. One regional agreement, the Western Climate Initiative, was launched in early 2007 and established a regional greenhouse gas reduction target shared by seven States.[8] The agreement calls for an economy- wide regional cap-and-trade program, the design of which will be publicly proposed in July 2008.[9] The latest U.S. regional agreement to be negotiated, the Midwestern Regional Greenhouse Gas Reduction Accord, commits another six States to near- and long-term greenhouse gas reduction goals under of a multi-sector cap-and-trade system. [10]

States are entering into regional partnerships to address climate change. One regional agreement, the Western Climate Initiative, was launched in early 2007 and established a regional greenhouse gas reduction target shared by seven States.[12] The agreement calls for an economy- wide regional cap-and-trade program, the design of which will be publicly proposed in July 2008.[13] The latest U.S. regional agreement to be negotiated, the Midwestern Regional Greenhouse Gas Reduction Accord, commits another six States to near- and long-term greenhouse gas reduction goals using a multi-sector cap-and-trade system. [14

In developing these regional agreements, as well as some cap-and-trade proposals within individual States,[15] there is recognition of the limits to the geographical and economic coverage of these market-based systems. Original agreement language and/or market advisory reports have repeatedly emphasized the need to address emissions leakage (migration of emissions activity outside regulated boundaries) and the potential for greater cost effectiveness of reductions in a larger system. [16]

State and Local Participation in Selected Climate Change Initiatives

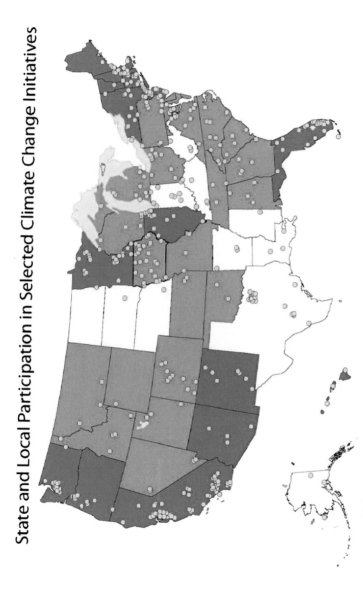

■ States with Greenhouse Gas Emission Targets and Participating in the Climate Registry (17)

■ States Participating in the Climate Registry without a Greenhouse Gas Emissions Target (22)

○ Cities Participating in the U.S. Mayors' Climate Protection Agreement (780)

Figure 1.[11].State and local participation in selected climate change initiatives.

Many State and local initiatives target the largest greenhouse gas emitting sector, electricity generation. Ten Northeastern and Mid-Atlantic States have joined the Regional Greenhouse Gas Initiative (RGGI), which was formed in 2003 to establish a power-sector emissions trading program.[17] The first RGGI three-year compliance period begins in 2009, with an initial public auctioning of allowances scheduled for June 2008. Implementing regulations and legislation are still pending, but informal accounting of commitments made by officials in the RGGI States indicates that a majority are planning to auction 100 percent of CO2 allowances. [18]

In 2002, California enacted the Nation's first greenhouse gas emission performance standard for power generation (SB 1368), which operates as a prerequisite for entering into longterm contracts to sell power within the State.[19] Other States face rising public demand to account for greenhouse gas emissions in power plant permitting, and in October 2007, Kansas became the first State to deny a coal-fired power plant construction permit based on the threat to public health and the environment from greenhouse gas emissions. [20]

Many other State and local initiatives that should have the co-benefit of reducing greenhouse gas emissions from the electricity sector were adopted for other reasons, including energy security, consumer protection, air quality benefits, or to attract capital investment in clean energy technologies. For example, 26 States plus the District of Columbia have established mandatory renewable electricity standards, and 34 States (plus D.C.) have implemented net metering policies (encouraging distributed generation by allowing utility customers with on-site renewable energy sources to sell power back to the grid).[21]

State and local governments also have programs to improve energy efficiency of power supply and end use. Fourteen States have set energy efficiency standards for utilities.[22] In 1978, California debuted a mechanism to decouple natural gas sales from utility revenue calculations in regulatory ratemaking; this approach was extended to electricity regulation in 1982. California's Public Utility Commission credits the decoupling policy with making California the nation's most energy efficient State.[23] At least nine other States have implemented or are considering similar policies.[24] States may also set efficiency standards for appliances that have no existing Federal standard, which 11 States have done.[25]

State and local governments can reduce greenhouse gas emissions by reducing the carbon footprint of their buildings and operations (including schools, hospitals, sewage treatment plants, municipal landfills, airports, bus fleets and terminals, street lighting and stop lights). For example, King County, Washington, recently announced plans to purchase 500 new hybrid buses over the next 5 years as part of its effort to convert the County's entire transit and vehicle fleet to low-emission vehicles.[26] One report found that State and local agencies collectively account for more than 75 percent of American government purchasing, and they could reap more than $1 billion in savings through energy efficient procurement.[27] The Federal Government is required to purchase energy-efficient products certified by either the ENERGY STAR label or the Federal Energy Management Program (FEMP); more than 15 States and 6 major cities serving over 40 percent of the U.S. population have adopted these same procurement practices.[28]

State and local governments also are using incentives to help their citizens reduce their carbon footprint. For example, Nassau County, New York, recently launched its "Green Levittown" initiative, a public-private partnership to reduce carbon emissions from Levittown homes by 20 percent in 2008 by helping residents conduct home energy audits, replace old boilers, and make other home energy savings improvements.[29] Arlington County, Virginia, is encouraging energy audits and energy efficiency improvements by its County residents and commercial buildings.[30] Some States and local governments also provide tax or other incentives for hybrid cars.

State governments have also adopted or are exploring regulatory programs to reduce greenhouse gas emissions from the transportation sector. In January 2007, California issued an executive order requiring its agencies to establish a low carbon fuel standard as the nation's first performance standard for greenhouse gas emissions from fuels.[31] Final promulgation of the standard is expected in December 2008. California has also attempted to regulate motor vehicle greenhouse gas emissions, and 16 additional States have moved to adopt California's standards.[32] At present, States cannot enforce these standards, however, because the Environmental Protection Agency (EPA) has announced it will deny California's petition for a waiver of preemption.[33]

State and/or local governments can also significantly affect greenhouse gas emissions through land use and transportation decisions. Much of the transportation network is managed by State and local governments, including the provision of public transit services, bicycle lanes, and pedestrian pathways to encourage more energy efficient travel. Transportation emissions are highly correlated with vehicle miles traveled (VMT), a parameter that State and local governments are particularly well-positioned to affect. Smart land use planning can reduce VMT while raising property values and the attractiveness of communities. For example, the city of Portland, Oregon, included in its greenhouse gas emission reduction strategy a target of reducing per-capita VMT 10 percent below 1995 levels by 2010, through a series of improved public transit and compact development zoning proposals.[34] Studies of other American metropolitan areas report the potential for 3 percent to as much as 25 percent reductions in VMT if State and local governments adopt smart growth planning strategies.[35] While greenhouse gas emission reductions may be a motivating factor, the attendant improvements in local and regional air quality are usually of substantial economic importance as well.

The Clean Air Act is one environmental statute that assigns different roles in different parts of the program to Federal, State, Tribal, and local governments.[36] This demonstrates some of the options available for different divisions of responsibility among governmental levels for standard setting, implementation, and enforcement. These options should help inform the Committee as it designs an approach for climate change.

The cornerstone of the Clean Air Act is the program for setting and meeting national ambient air quality standards (NAAQS) for the most widespread types of air pollution. That program uses a "cooperative federalism" approach to bring air pollution (such as smog and soot) down to a level that protects public health with an adequate margin of safety. EPA sets health- based ambient air quality standards after an exhaustive review of the available science, and States have primary responsibility for attaining those standards. Each State generally has the obligation to decide which sources to regulate and the extent to which each will be regulated so that air quality in the State meets the national health-based standard, although EPA sets minimum emission limits for some pollution sources and minimum requirements for State programs.

Generally, the Clean Air Act requires EPA to establish national emission limits for the most significant national stationary sources of air pollution. For many stationary sources (e.g., industrial facilities), EPA sets performance requirements.[37] The Clean Air Act, however, clearly states that nothing in the Act shall preclude or deny the right of any State or political subdivision to set more stringent requirements.[38] By regulating sources within their borders, States can provide their citizens with additional local public health or environmental protection, spur technology development, or try to move the country towards more stringent standards. Some States have adopted regulations more stringent than Federal law, but other States have laws that prevent the State environmental agency from adopting regulations that are more stringent than the Federal requirements.[39]

Responsibility for enforcement of Clean Air Act controls on stationary sources is generally shared by EPA and State, Tribal, or local governments. State, Tribal, and local governments are usually the primary regulatory contacts for the majority of regulated stationary sources. Requirements in State implementation plans for meeting national air quality standards are enforced primarily by the State or political jurisdiction responsible for the plan. States also implement the Clean Air Act's permitting programs, so States take the lead in issuing construction and operating permits and enforcing the requirements in those permits. EPA may also enforce requirements in State plans and permits after providing notice to the relevant State.

The Clean Air Act does not allow a State to regulate stationary sources outside its borders even if the emissions from those sources cause environmental or public health problems in that State. To achieve that result, Federal intervention is required. EPA can regulate those sources (or require regulation by the sources' home State) if EPA determines that those sources are significantly contributing to the State's violation of Federal air quality standards.[40]

Environmental problems caused by emissions in other States led to Congressional adoption of the Acid Rain Trading Program, which controlled power plants emissions that were causing acid rain many miles downwind. For the Acid Rain Trading Program, Congress set the cap level in the 1990 Clean Air Act Amendments. EPA both implements and enforces the program, although States have authority to enforce the monitoring requirements. When the Acid Rain program was added in 1990, it was layered on top of the existing air pollution structure described above. This structure was important because the pollutants that cause acid rain also cause air pollution that contributes to local and regional public health problems. Each State has the right to impose more stringent requirements on power plants within its borders. The more stringent requirements can be specific performance standards that apply to the plants or a requirement to turn in more than one allowance per ton emitted. A State cannot, however, impose more stringent requirements on plants outside of its borders or interfere with the free trade of allowances.[41]

The Clean Air Act took a different approach on mobile sources, where there are greater concerns about burdens on interstate commerce. The Clean Air Act requires EPA to set standards for new motor vehicles and prohibits States and political subdivisions from adopting more stringent standards except in limited circumstances. In recognition of its early role in regulating vehicle emissions to address that State's serious and unique local air pollution problems, the Act allows California to adopt and enforce more stringent standards for new motor vehicles if it obtains approval from EPA. [42] Other States may adopt and enforce California's standards, but cannot adopt different standards.[43] The Clean Air Act follows the same basic approach for most new and used nonroad vehicles and engines.[44]

Under the Act, States and political subdivisions are prohibited from adopting or enforcing emission standards for aircraft, engines below 175 horsepower for farm and construction equipment, and new locomotives unless the standards are identical to the Federal standards.[45]

The Act also limits States' ability to regulate transportation fuel (i.e., fuel used by highway and nonroad vehicles and engines). EPA sets standards for transportation fuel to control emissions from the use of the fuel. Except for California, States and political subdivisions are prohibited from setting or enforcing standards for fuel components or characteristics for the purpose of motor vehicle emission control if (1) EPA has determined that no control of that component or characteristic is necessary under the Act or (2) EPA has regulated that component or characteristic.[46] Until 2005, a State could avoid that prohibition only if EPA determined that State regulation was necessary for that State to attain the health- based air quality standards. Due to concern about "boutique fuels," State authority was limited further in the Energy Policy Act of 2005. It amended the Clean Air Act by limiting the number of different State fuels to those previously approved by EPA.[47]

In recognition of the States' role in achieving our national air quality goals, EPA provides grant money to States to help them run State air programs. Starting with fiscal year 2007, the President's Budget Request has proposed a $30 million (15 percent) decrease in funding from 2006 levels. In recognition of the important role played by State and local air quality agencies in meeting our air quality goals, the Committee and Subcommittee Chairmen and other Members of this Committee have opposed the decrease in funding.[48]

The 1990 Clean Air Act Amendments added a new program to address the global problem of protecting the stratospheric ozone layer from depletion by the release of chemical substances. This program was designed to meet our obligations under the Montreal Protocol. The stratospheric ozone program is a comprehensive, entirely Federal program governing the production, importation, consumption, exportation, disposal, and labeling of ozone-depleting substances.

RATIONALIZING GOVERNMENTAL ROLES

Meeting the challenge posed by climate change will require the involvement of all levels of government. As the Committee designs a comprehensive, national climate change program, it will need to address the questions of what roles are best played by each level of government and how these roles should be reflected in Federal climate change legislation. For different parts of the program, different roles will be appropriate. This Paper is designed to help frame future deliberations and dialogue by discussing some of the key factors that should be considered and balanced as the Committee moves forward.

Rationalizing governmental roles requires an examination of which level of government is best suited for each role so that we can efficiently achieve the national goal of reducing greenhouse gas emissions by 60 to 80 percent by 2050. This is a broader question than just whether, or under what circumstances, it is appropriate for States, Tribes, or localities to set their own standards apart from the Federal program. Some bills introduced in Congress would allow State, Tribal, and local governments to adopt controls more stringent than the national requirements. A number of factors should be considered in determining whether that is the right approach. One key distinction between climate change and most other environmental problems is that climate change is a global, not local, problem, perhaps providing less need for allowing States to be more stringent. More stringent State programs might unduly burden interstate commerce or increase the governmental or societal resources needed to achieve the necessary reductions. Different States or regions of the country might also have different interests that should be balanced at a national level. On the other hand, more stringent State programs could achieve additional levels of reductions, spur technology development, test new programs, or reduce the cost of achieving the level of national reductions sufficient to stabilize global atmospheric greenhouse gas concentrations.

Careful attention will need to be paid to the interaction between potential State, Tribal, and/or local programs and the use of a national, economy-wide cap-and-trade program as the cornerstone of our climate change approach. Under most environmental programs, a more stringent State program provides additional environmental or public health protection. With a national cap-and-trade program, though, a more stringent State program may just shift the location of, rather than decrease, national emissions because the sources subject to the more stringent State program will need fewer allowances (thus freeing up allowances for sources in other States). Unlike most air pollutants, local greenhouse gas reductions alone will not help the local area given that climate change is caused by global, rather than local, concentrations of greenhouse gases. Consideration also needs to be given to how State programs would affect the cost of reducing greenhouse gas emissions and on who would bear that cost. Some of these issues are touched upon later in this chapter, but will need further exploration.

Please note that the sections below discuss each factor separately and provide examples of how that factor might apply to a particular part of a comprehensive national climate change program. This chapter is intended to provide insight into important considerations for determining appropriate governmental roles. It is not a comprehensive discussion of how all of these factors would apply to any particular aspect of the climate change program, nor does it address how the Committee should balance these different factors. To the extent that specific programs are discussed, the purpose of this Paper is to help the reader understand how a specific factor might apply.

The Global Effect of Greenhouse Gas Emissions

One key factor that distinguishes climate change from other pollution problems our country has tackled is that local greenhouse gas emissions do not cause local environmental or health problems, except to the extent that the emissions contribute to global atmospheric concentrations. This characteristic of greenhouse gases stands in contrast to most pollution problems, where emissions adversely affect people locally where the emissions occur. The global nature of climate change takes away (or at least greatly minimizes) one of the primary reasons many national environmental programs have provisions preserving State authority to adopt and enforce environmental programs that are more stringent than Federal programs: States have a responsibility to protect their own citizens. This reality does not, however, lead to the conclusion that States, Tribes, or localities should not do anything to address climate change. As discussed elsewhere in this chapter, there are other reasons why it is essential that State, Tribal, and local governments participate in combating climate change.

Effect on the Level and Cost of National Greenhouse Gas Emissions

The effect of State, Tribal, or local programs on the level of national greenhouse gas emissions and the cost of reductions are factors to consider in rationalizing governmental roles.[49] The use of a national, economy-wide cap-and-trade program as the cornerstone of our country's approach to climate change requires careful consideration of the effect of State, Tribal, or local programs on both national emissions and cost. With most Federal environmental programs, more stringent local programs reduce national emissions. That result is not necessarily achieved with a Federal cap-and-trade program. State, Tribal, and local programs may either decrease or not change national greenhouse gas emissions, and either increase, not change, or decrease the cost of achieving reductions. The effect will depend on several design elements of both the Federal cap-and-trade program (including its scope and whether it has a hard or soft cap) and the State, Tribal, or local program.

Therefore, questions that should be asked are:

- In the presence of a national cap-and-trade greenhouse gas program and other Federal requirements, will a particular State, Tribal, or local program reduce national greenhouse gas emissions?
- In the presence of a national cap-and-trade greenhouse gas program and other Federal requirements, how will a particular State, Tribal, or local program affect costs and who bears the costs?

To help explain how different programs might affect national emissions and allowance prices, this section reviews several hypothetical scenarios. The scenarios are not meant to be exhaustive, but rather are illustrative of the careful analysis required to determine the effect of State, Tribal, and local programs.

Figure 2 and the accompanying table show several hypothetical scenarios as a way of demonstrating how different types of State, Tribal, and local programs might affect the national level of greenhouse gas emissions and the cost of reducing emissions, assuming that the Federal cap-and-trade program had a hard cap on emissions.[50]

- Case A (Figure 2) shows a hypothetical Federal cap-and-trade program that is perfectly efficient and, thus, achieves all the most cost-effective reductions.
- Case B (Figure 2), the Base Case, shows a hypothetical Federal cap-and-trade program that is more realistic and assumes that some of the cheapest reductions do not happen due to imperfections in the market.
- The reductions reflected in Cases A and B are identical, but the cost of Case B is higher because of the inefficiencies in the market.
- Case C (Figure 2) takes the Base Case, and adds a State, Tribal, or local program that corrects for some market inefficiencies and picks up low cost reductions that were missed by the Base Case. Local building codes might have this effect.
- Case C achieves the same reductions as the Base Case, but at a lower private sector cost (although probably with increased governmental costs to run the State, Tribal, or local program).
- Case D (Figure 2) takes the Base Case, and adds a State, Tribal, or local program that requires some reductions that are more expensive than the reductions that would otherwise occur under the Federal cap-and-trade program. State tailpipe vehicle regulations might have this effect.

- Case D achieves the same reductions as the Base Case, but at a higher private sector cost (and probably with increased governmental costs to run the State, Tribal, or local program).
- Case E (Figure 2) takes the Base Case, and adds a State, Tribal, or local program that requires reductions that would occur anyway under the Federal program. This might be the case for a State cap-and-trade program covering a subset of the entities covered by the Federal program.
- Case E achieves the same reductions as the Base Case with the same private sector costs (although there may be increased transaction costs for the private sector and increased governmental costs).
- Case F (Figure 2) takes the Base Case, and adds a State, Tribal, or local program that requires reduction of emissions that are outside the cap.[51]
- Case F achieves greater reductions than the Base Case. The costs could go up or down depending on whether the required emission reductions had a negative or positive cost.
-

In summary, if there is a hard Federal cap on greenhouse gas emissions, a State, Tribal, or local program lowering emissions from a sector or locality covered by the cap generally frees up allowances that can be used by someone in another sector or locality. As a result, the State, Tribal, or local program will not decrease national emissions and its effect on cost and allowance prices will depend on the program. In contrast, a State, Tribal, or local program lowering emissions from a sector completely outside the cap will decrease national emissions.

It has been suggested that States that adopt greenhouse gas programs (for emissions covered by the cap) should be able to retire allowances equal to a program's expected reductions.[52] This is based on the theory that States should have the option of reducing national emissions (by retiring allowances) if they want to adopt a program more stringent than the Federal program, although this raises the question of what it means for a program to be "more stringent" if it requires reductions in emissions that are covered by the national cap.

Retiring allowances would mean that local programs would decrease national emissions. It is unclear, however, how this would affect the cost of the program, particularly for citizens of other States.

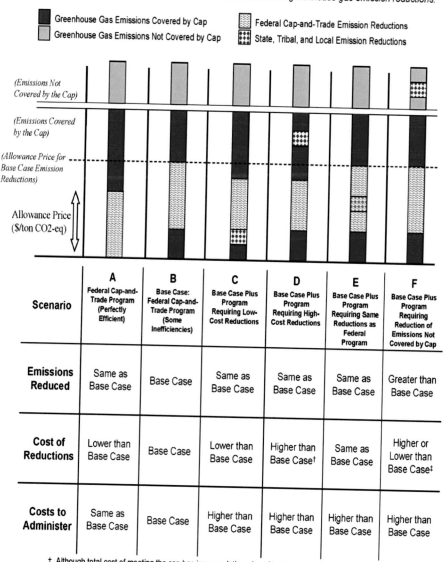

Figure 2. Possible effects of state, tribal, and local programs on cost and level of emission reductions (hard cap).

- For example, in Case E (Figure 2), where the reductions from the State, Tribal, or local program would occur anyway under the Federal program, retiring allowances would likely increase allowance prices and compliance costs nationally (compared to the Base Case).
- In contrast, in Case C (Figure 2), where reductions from the State, Tribal, or local program are cheaper than the reductions that would occur under the Federal program, retiring allowances would likely result in allowance prices and national compliance costs equal to the Base Case.

The previous discussion assumed that the Federal cap was a hard cap. The analysis differs (and gets more complicated), however, if one assumes Federal legislation with a soft cap. (A program would have a soft cap if it included a safety valve that required the government to sell an unlimited number of allowances when allowance prices hit a specified price.) Figure 3 and its accompanying table show several hypothetical scenarios based on this assumption.

- Case A (Figure 3) shows a hypothetical Federal cap-and-trade program that is perfectly
- efficient and, thus, achieves all the most cost-effective reductions.
- Case B (Fig. 3), the Base Case, shows a hypothetical Federal cap-and-trade program that is more realistic and assumes both that some of the cheapest reductions do not happen due to imperfections in the market and that, as a result, the safety valve is triggered.
- Case B (Base Case) achieves fewer emission reductions and has a higher allowance price than Case A.
- Case C (Fig. 3) takes the Base Case, and adds a State, Tribal, or local program that corrects for some market inefficiencies and picks up low cost reductions that were missed by the Base Case. Local building codes might have this effect.
- Case C achieves greater emission reductions than the Base Case, and would have identical or lower allowance prices.
- Case D (Fig. 3) takes the Base Case, and adds a State, Tribal, or local program that requires some reductions that are more expensive than the reductions that would otherwise occur under the Federal cap-and-trade program. State tailpipe vehicle regulations might have this effect.
- Case D achieves greater emission reductions than the Base Case, at an identical or lower allowance price.

Assuming there is a Federal cap-and-trade program with a safety valve, this figure illustrates the possible effects of hypothetical State, Tribal, and local programs on the cost and level of greenhouse gas emission reductions.

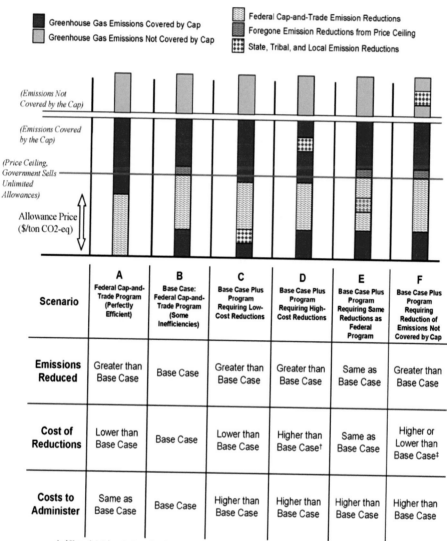

Figure 3. Possible effects of state, tribal, and local programs on cost and level of emission reductions (cap with safety valve).

- Case E (Fig. 3) takes the Base Case, and adds a State, Tribal, or local program that requires reductions that would occur anyway under the Federal program. This might be the case for a State cap-and-trade program covering a subset of the entities covered by the Federal program.
- Case E achieves the same reductions as the Base Case with the same allowance prices.
- Case F (Fig. 3) takes the Base Case, and adds a State, Tribal, or local program that requires reduction of emissions that are outside the cap.[53]
- Case F achieves greater reductions than the Base Case at identical allowance prices.

The preceding discussion, which looked at only a select number of hypothetical scenarios, demonstrates that careful analysis will be required to determine how national emissions and allowance prices would be affected by State, Tribal, and local programs that limit greenhouse gas emissions that are covered by a national cap.

Efficient Use of Government and Societal Resources

The challenge posed by climate change is daunting. Unfortunately, the enormity of the challenge makes it more likely that too few, rather than too many, resources will be available to meet the challenges of reducing greenhouse gases and adapting to whatever climate change is not prevented. Given the likelihood of limited resources, it is important to use both government and societal resources efficiently. In trying to rationalize governmental roles for any particular aspect of the climate change program, at least two questions should be asked:

- Does the approach increase or decrease the use of government resources needed to achieve the same level of greenhouse gas reductions?
- Does the approach increase or decrease the use of non-government resources needed to achieve the same level of greenhouse gas reductions?

Some State, Tribal, and local programs could significantly improve the efficiency of societal resources used to achieve the necessary greenhouse gas reductions. This effect is most pronounced for programs that achieve reductions that a cap-and-trade program either would not cover or would miss due to market imperfections.[54] For example, the economically rational choice may be to install better insulation in a new home because the increased purchase price of the new home would be more than offset by future decreases in electricity and heating bills (compared to the same home with standard insulation). The market may not achieve this result, however, even if the cap-and-trade program is broad enough to incorporate the price of carbon into electricity, natural gas, and heating oil provided to residential customers. Home builders may have a disincentive to put in better insulation because home buyers generally are more sensitive to a home's purchase price than to future electricity and heating bills. State, Tribal, or local building codes could capture these otherwise lost or uncovered emission reductions, and thereby decrease the societal cost of achieving greenhouse gas reductions.

Even in a national cap-and-trade program, certain partnership approaches between the Federal Government and State, Tribal, or local governments may optimize the use of government resources. A cap-and-trade program requires accurate monitoring and recordkeeping. It is probably more efficient to authorize State, Tribal, and/or local governments to inspect sources to determine compliance with national monitoring and record-keeping requirements than it would be to leave that exclusively to Federal inspectors. States currently inspect sources to determine compliance with existing air pollution and other environmental requirements (including compliance with Acid Rain Trading Program monitoring requirements). Adding a climate change program to their inspection list is probably a more efficient use of governmental resources than allowing only Federal inspectors to check compliance with those requirements.

On the other hand, once a national, economy-wide cap-and-trade program is adopted, State or regional cap-and-trade programs may interfere with the efficient functioning of the Federal cap-and-trade program and increase demands on both governmental and non-governmental resources.[55] If there are multiple programs, multiple government agencies will be expending resources on those cap-and-trade programs without necessarily achieving more greenhouse gas reductions than a single national program. With a national, economy-wide cap on emissions, a more stringent State or regional cap might shift emissions from the more stringent State to other States, without reducing national greenhouse gas emissions.[56] In this scenario, requiring regulated entities to comply with multiple cap-and-trade programs (which would likely require different compliance strategies) would likely increase the expenditure of non-governmental resources (as compared to having just one national program) without reducing greenhouse gas emissions. For example, a regulated entity might have to buy both State and Federal allowances to cover the same ton of greenhouse gas emissions. Different points of regulation or allocation methodologies between State and Federal programs would also cause complications and increase resources necessary for compliance.

If there is a hard Federal cap that includes the transportation sector, State adoption of California's vehicle greenhouse gas standards would increase private sector resources necessary to achieve that cap due to the administrative burdens associated with meeting multiple State programs. Because manufacturers would be required to ensure that the fleet they sold in each State met the fleet-wide average required under California's program, they would have additional administrative burdens to track vehicle sales and, perhaps, control the types or numbers of vehicles sold in each State. (Normally vehicle mixes vary by region, so designing a fleet to meet California's fleet average would not necessarily ensure that the fleet would meet that same average in Rhode Island or Vermont or any other State.)

The Benefit of States, Tribes, and Localities as Laboratories

For many emerging issues, State and local governments play an important role as laboratories in which to develop political consensus, design and test new programs, and spur technology development. In developing national climate change legislation, there are two different parts of this role that need to be recognized. First, States and localities have already been active in addressing climate change and the national legislation needs to be informed by their efforts. Second, in determining the appropriate roles of each level of government, the Committee should consider the benefit of States, Tribes, and localities serving as laboratories in the future as part of the national approach to climate change.

State and local governments are playing an important role in developing and demonstrating a national political consensus that this country needs mandatory measures to reduce greenhouse gas emissions. The level of activity on climate change at the State and local level is one of the key drivers for national legislation on climate change.

In designing national climate change legislation, the committee can benefit from lessons learned by State and local government efforts taken in the absence of Federal action. For example, the Congressional debate on allowance distributions has and will continue to be informed by the work done by the States in RGGI. California's Market Advisory Committee Report is an important compendium of information for designing carbon markets. California's work on a low carbon transportation fuel standard helped influence the lifecycle greenhouse gas requirements in the renewable fuel standard in last year's energy bill.

Once Federal climate change legislation is enacted and implemented, there is still a need for State, Tribal, and local governments to act as laboratories, but the nature of their role as laboratories changes. In rationalizing governmental roles, one question that should be asked is:

- For particular types of programs, would State, Tribal, or local governments be acting as laboratories and would that be beneficial?

The answer to this question may depend on the circumstances. For example, a State probably would not be acting as a laboratory for testing new policies or driving technology development if it mandated that refiners sell a certain amount of renewable transportation fuel (such as ethanol). The Federal Government already has such a mandate, and a State mandate would only affect the location of sales of renewable fuels, not the national total amount sold. A State or locality, however, might be acting as a laboratory if it enacted a requirement for E85 as part of a comprehensive plan to increase E85 use and distribution networks.

The benefit of California as a laboratory for air pollution requirements is often cited by proponents as a reason for allowing California to adopt its own motor vehicle standards. California's passenger vehicle standards for traditional air pollutants have spurred the development of better emission-control technologies that have helped reduce air pollution across the country, although EPA has traditionally led in setting heavy-duty vehicle standards.[57] California has provided a benefit as a laboratory even when its results have not been positive; California's unsuccessful electric vehicle mandate was not adopted at the Federal level.

Using California as a laboratory might play out differently for greenhouse gas emissions than it has for traditional air pollutants. At the moment, greenhouse gas emissions can be limited by fundamentally changing the characteristics of the vehicles (e.g., size, materials, performance). Unlike the situation for reducing criteria pollutants from vehicle tailpipe emissions, currently there is no aftertreatment technology to control carbon dioxide tailpipe emissions. There is enormous investment in yet-unproven technologies (e.g., plug-in hybrids, fuel cells) that may or may not prove commercially viable.

It should be noted that when other States representing a significant share of the new vehicle market adopt the California standards, those States are going beyond the role of laboratories for testing a new policy or new technology that could then be adopted nationally if it were proven effective. Rather, those States are effectively skipping the laboratory stage and going straight to setting new national standards.

States, Tribes, and localities may also continue to serve as laboratories for developing political consensus by adopting more stringent programs in the future. Pressure would build for the Federal Government to adopt or strengthen regulations as more States, Tribes, or localities adopt more stringent, but not necessarily identical, programs.

Differing Local Circumstances

Circumstances that are relevant to good program design and that differ significantly across the country are likely to be a factor in favor of a primary or solo role for State, Tribal, or local governments, or a partnership approach with the Federal Government playing a limited role. In trying to rationalize governmental roles, one question that should be asked is:

- To what extent does the design of this component of the climate change program depend on circumstances that differ across the country?

For example, building codes should depend significantly on circumstances that differ across the country, including weather conditions and the amount of new construction. This consideration weighs in favor of State, Tribal, or local governments playing the primary role in establishing building codes. The Federal Government might have a role to play in setting minimum standards, providing information on the benefits of different building code requirements, or providing some funding,[58] but the differing local circumstances would weigh against the Federal Government having sole control over building codes.

Adaptation to the climate change we do not prevent will also be very dependent on local circumstances because different parts of the country will experience different effects. Some climate change effects pose unique challenges to specific economies and cultures within the U.S., such as the projected loss of sugar maples in the Northeast or the melting of permafrost undermining structural foundations in Alaskan communities. Other repercussions will further complicate regional management of natural resources, such as changes in the timing and amount of freshwater availability in the West due to decreasing snowpack. Even for widespread effects such as sea level rise, different areas must adapt to different challenges; the Southeast is especially prone to loss of coastal wetlands and thus increased storm surge.[59] State, Tribal, and local governments will need to play a major role in developing and implementing adaptation strategies, although the Federal Government will also have a role to play.

In contrast, monitoring and reporting of greenhouse gas emissions should not be dependent on local circumstances. In fact, a national cap-and-trade program would be undermined if monitoring standards or reporting timetables (for example) varied by State or locality. This consideration weighs in favor of a primary or sole role for the Federal Government in setting monitoring standards and reporting timetables (although State, Tribal, and local governments may be best suited to ensure compliance).

Burden on Interstate Commerce

If a patchwork of State or local programs would impose a burden on interstate commerce that causes inefficient or wasteful resource allocation, that factor would weigh in favor of the Federal Government having the exclusive or primary role for this part of a comprehensive climate change program. To rationalize governmental roles, two questions should be asked:

- For any particular component of a comprehensive climate change program, what burden, if any, would multiple State, Tribal, and local programs impose on interstate commerce?
- Are there ways to reduce such a burden?

A burden on interstate commerce is most likely to be a problem for products that are sold across State lines, such as transportation fuel. A State biofuels program that sets lifecycle greenhouse gas reductions requirements that are more stringent than the Federal requirements would likely burden interstate commerce. Fuel providers would have to make sure that a sufficient supply of State fuel was available. In case of unexpected refinery outages or distribution problems for that State, fuel providers could not easily reroute fuel from other States to cover the special State market.

In contrast, programs that focus on land use issues are unlikely to pose a significant burden on interstate commerce. Regulation of emissions from stationary sources (such as industrial facilities) within a State's jurisdiction is also unlikely to pose a significant burden on interstate commerce.

The Imposition of Burdens on other States

In deciding whether States, Tribes, or localities should be able to adopt programs that achieve greater greenhouse gas reductions, one key factor is whether the cost or other economic burden will be borne by the State that adopts the program or by other States. Many programs will have no or minimal incidental effects outside the jurisdictions that adopt them, which would weigh in favor of States, Tribes, and localities having the option to adopt those programs. Some programs, however, may have detrimental effects on other States, such as increased costs or other economic burdens, which would be a factor weighing in favor of a sole or primary role for the Federal Government. One of the primary roles of the Federal Government is to provide a forum for resolving disputes between different States or regions of the country and balancing the competing interests at stake. One question that should be asked is:

- Is there concern that a particular program would impose a significant (or different) burden outside the State (or States) that have adopted it?

The California greenhouse gas tailpipe standards are an example of some States adopting a program that could impose a significant economic burden outside the boundaries of those States. If California and the other States that have adopted the California vehicle greenhouse gas standards were allowed to enforce those standards, they could effectively become national standards.[60] The States most dependent on domestic auto industry manufacturing have not adopted the California greenhouse gas vehicle standards (see Figure 4), yet they could be significantly affected by those standards if the domestic auto industry's concerns are borne out.[61] On the other hand, California has an interest in broadly adopted, more stringent greenhouse gas tailpipe standards. California adopted the standards in part based on its concern that it has unique climate change vulnerability due to a fragile water-supply system facing saltwater intrusion and decreasing snow pack, and that higher global temperatures will exacerbate California's ozone pollution.[62] This difference of State interests, and the mismatch between the States setting the standards and the States risking a significant economic burden, would be a factor weighing in favor of resolving the issue at the Federal level, rather than leaving the decision to individual States.[63]

In contrast, if a State were considering whether to require its local industry to meet a more stringent standard, the industry and its employees would have a voice in the political process leading up to the decision. Additionally, if the State is requiring its sources to make greenhouse gas reductions that are more expensive than what they would otherwise make, the State may be lowering the price of allowances nationally (and the cost of meeting the national cap) for sources in other States. In circumstances where a State decides to impose a burden on its own citizens and industry without imposing a significant burden outside the State, those circumstances would weigh in favor of a primary State role and a limited (if any) Federal role.

Stakeholder Needs

Passing national climate change legislation will require political consensus. State and local governments have already invested significant resources and political capital to develop climate change programs. The more time that elapses before enactment of Federal legislation, the less likely it is that they would agree to drop or modify their programs.[64] On the other hand, one of the main reasons industry would contribute to the consensus in support of a national program is to avoid a patchwork of State, Tribal, and local regulations.

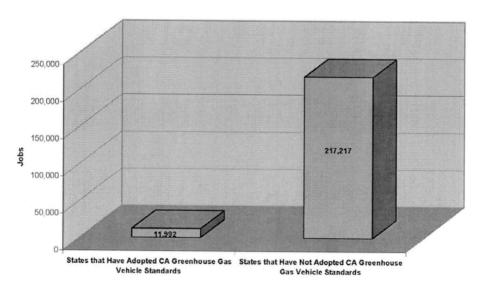

Figure 4. [65] Domestic automobile industry manufacturing jobs and stat adoption of California greenhouse gas vehicle standards.

Balancing These Factors

As the debate over whether the Federal Government should preempt California's greenhouse gas motor vehicle standards has shown, Committee Members balance these various factors in a way that can lead to different conclusions that will need to be worked out through the legislative process. Chairman Dingell has made it very clear that he believes that motor vehicle greenhouse gas standards should be set by the Federal Government, not by State governments: greenhouse gases are global (not local) pollutants, multiple programs would be an undue burden on interstate commerce and would waste societal and governmental resources without reducing national emissions, and the competing interests of different States should be resolved at the Federal level. Other Committee Members have reached the opposite conclusion given the severity of the climate change problem, the need to push technological development, and the benefits of having States act as laboratories.

Although some issues regarding appropriate roles for different levels of government may be contentious, for other issues (such as State inspection of monitoring equipment or local government's right to set more stringent building codes), balancing these factors may quickly lead Members to agreement.

CONCLUSION

The appropriate roles for Federal, State, Tribal, and local governments in a comprehensive, national approach to climate change will be affected by the design of the underlying approach. It is clear, however, that all levels of government must play a role (in fact, a variety of roles) in meeting this challenge. Rationalizing these roles as the climate change program is developed will require thoughtful and careful consideration and a balancing of a number of factors.

REFERENCES

[1]   The question of whether States, Tribes, or localities should be allocated allowances or allowance revenue is generally beyond the scope of this Paper.

[2]   Committee on Energy and Commerce, Subcommittee on Energy and Air Quality, "Climate Change: State and Local Perspectives" (March 15, 2007).

[3]   Office of the Governor of California, "Gov. Schwarzenegger Signs Landmark Legislation to Reduce Greenhouse Gas Emissions," (Sept. 27, 2006), http://climatechange.ca.gov/documents/2006-09-27_AB32_GOV_ NEWS_RELEASE.PDF.

[4]   Legislation with greenhouse gas targets was signed into law in Hawaii, Maine, Minnesota, New Jersey, Oregon, and Washington. Governors have set targets in Arizona, Connecticut, Florida, Illinois, Massachusetts, New Hampshire, New Mexico, New York, Rhode Island, and Vermont. Source: Pew Center State Action Maps (accessed February 11, 2008), http://www.pewclimate.org/what_s_being_done/in_the_states/state_action_ maps.cfm.

[5]   US Conference of Mayors, "List of Participating Mayors" (accessed February 4, 2008), http://usmayors.org/climateprotection/list.asp.

[6]   Institute for Local Self-Reliance, "Lessons from the Pioneers: Tackling Global Warming at the Local Level" (Jan. 2007), p. 3, http://www.newrules.org/de/pioneers.pdf.

[7]   The Climate Registry (accessed February 11, 2008), http://www.theclimateregistry.org/.

[8]   The States fully participating are Arizona, California, Montana, New Mexico, Oregon, Utah, and Washington. The Western Climate Initiative (accessed February 11, 2008), http://www.westernclimateinitiative. org/Index.cfm.

[9]   A WCI workgroup for the electricity sector recently released an options paper for a stakeholder conference in January 2008 focused largely on selecting the point of regulation. WCI Electricity Subcommittee Options Paper (January 2, 2007), http://www.westernclimateinitiative.org /ewebeditpro/items/O104F14577.PDF.

[10] States fully participating include Illinois, Iowa, Kansas, Michigan, Minnesota, and Wisconsin. Office of the Governor of Wisconsin, "Ten Midwestern Leaders Sign Greenhouse Gas Accord" (November 15, 2007), http://www.wisgov.state.wi.us/journal_media_detail.asp?locid=19&prid=30 27. The agreement calls for a 30-month implementation timeframe with the formulation of greenhouse gas reduction targets to be announced later this year. Midwestern Greenhouse Gas Reduction Accord (accessed February 11, 2008), http://www.wisgov.state.wi.us/docview.asp?docid=12497.

[11] Information in this figure was taken from the Climate Registry, the Pew Center on Climate Change, and the US Conference of Mayors.

[12] The States fully participating are Arizona, California, Montana, New Mexico, Oregon, Utah, and Washington. The Western Climate Initiative

(accessed February 11, 2008), http://www.westernclimateinitiative. org/Index.cfm.

[13] A WCI workgroup for the electricity sector recently released an options paper for a stakeholder conference in January 2008 focused largely on selecting the point of regulation. WCI Electricity Subcommittee Options Paper (January 2, 2007), http://www.westernclimateinitiative. org/ewebeditpro/items/O104F14577.PDF.

[14] States fully participating include Illinois, Iowa, Kansas, Michigan, Minnesota, and Wisconsin. Office of the Governor of Wisconsin, "Ten Midwestern Leaders Sign Greenhouse Gas Accord" (November 15, 2007), http://www.wisgov.state.wi.us /journal_media_detail.asp?locid=19&prid=3027. The agreement calls for a 30-month implementation timeframe with the formulation of greenhouse gas reduction targets to be announced later this year. Midwestern Greenhouse Gas Reduction Accord (accessed February 11, 2008), http://www.wisgov.state.wi.us/docview.asp?docid=12497.

[15] Florida was recently advised by its Governor's Action Team on Energy and Climate Change that a cap-and-trade system would be "a vital component" to meet the Governor's cap on utility emissions and overall greenhouse gas emission reduction goals. Florida Department of Environmental Protection, "Straw Findings and Recommendations" (October 5, 2007), p. 5, http://www.dep. state.fl.us/ClimateChange/team/file/2007_1005_adams.pdf.

[16] See, e.g., Market Advisory Committee to the California Air Resources Board, "Recommendations for Designing a Greenhouse Gas Cap-and-Trade System for California" (June 30, 2007), p. 52, http://www.climatechange. ca.gov/documents/2007-06-29_MAC_FINAL_REPORT.PDF.

[17] States participating in the cap-and-trade market include Connecticut, Delaware, Maine, Maryland, Massachusetts, New Hampshire, New Jersey, New York, Rhode Island, and Vermont. The Regional Greenhouse Gas Initiative (accessed February 11, 2008), http://www.rggi.org/.

[18] Conversation with Dallas Burtraw at Resources for the Future.

[19] California Energy Commission, "SB 1368 Emission Performance Standards" (accessed February 11, 2008), http://www.energy.ca.gov /emission_standards/index.html.

[20] The Washington Post, "Power Plant Rejected Over Carbon Dioxide For First Time" (October 19, 2007), http://www.washingtonpost.com/wp-dyn/content/article/2007/10/18/AR2007101802452.html.

[21] Pew Center opera cit.

[22] Ibid.

[23] California Public Utility Commission, "California's Decoupling Policy" (accessed February 11, 2008), http://www.cpuc.ca.gov/cleanenergy /design/docs/Deccouplinglowres.pdf.

[24] 24 Regulatory Assistance Project, "Barriers and Incentives: Enabling Energy Efficiency" (October 29, 2007), p. 62, http://www.raponline.org /Feature.asp?select=78&Submit1=Submit.

[25] Pew Center opera cit.

[26] Climate Communities, "Climate Action from the Ground Up: Agenda for Federal Action" (accessed February 14, 2008), p. 2, http://www.climatecommunities.us/pdf/ccFederalActionAgenda.pdf.

[27] 27 Alliance to Save Energy, "US Experience with Energy-Efficient Procurement at the State and Local Levels" (July 13-14, 2007), p. 5, http://www.asiapacificpartnership.org/BATFenergyefficiencyworkshop.htm

[28] Ibid p. 12.

[29] Climate Communities opera cit.

[30] Ibid.

[31] California Energy Commission, "The Low Carbon Fuel Standard" (accessed February 11, 2008), http://www.energy.ca.gov/low_carbon_fuel_standard/.

[32] Pew Center opera cit.

[33] Letter from EPA Administrator Johnson to California Governor Schwarzenegger (December 19, 2007), http://www.epa.gov/otaq/climate/20071219-slj.pdf.

[34] 34Center for Clean Air Policy, "Transportation Emissions Guidebook" (accessed February 11, 2008), p. 86, http://www.ccap.org/safe /guidebook/guide_complete.html.

[35] Ibid p. 83.

[36] The discussion in this section highlights some key aspects of the Clean Air Act, but it is not a comprehensive review.

[37] For example, section 111 of the Clean Air Act authorizes EPA to set New Source Performance Standards (NSPS), intended to drive cost-effective adoption of the best available air pollution control technologies in newly constructed sources. Section 112 of the Act also requires EPA to set Maximum Achievable Control Technology (MACT) standards for affected sources to limit emissions of hazardous air pollutants through tailored industry-specific control measures.

[38] Clean Air Act Sec. 116.

[39] Possibly the most restrictive, Pennsylvania's "Regulatory Basics Initiative" requires amendment of any State regulation to be no more stringent than its Federal counterpart. State Environmental Resource Center, "'No More

Stringent' Laws" (March 26, 2004), http://www.serconline.org/ noMoreStringent.html. A 2002 survey of State agencies reported that 26 States were partially or wholly precluded, due to State laws or policies, from setting stricter standards related to the Clean Air Act. Only 14 States reported adopting more stringent standards at a rate higher than "infrequently." STAPPA-ALAPCO, "Restrictions on the Stringency of State and Local Air Quality Programs" (December 17, 2002), pp. 1-2, http://www.4cleanair.org/stringency-report.pdf.

[40] Clean Air Act Secs. 1 10(a)(2)(D) and 126. EPA used this authority when it issued the Clean Air Interstate Rule (CAIR) to limit regional sulfur dioxide (SO2) and nitrogen oxide (NOx) emissions to help States meet the ozone and fine particle standards. Federal Register, "Clean Air Interstate Rule," Vol. 70, No. 91 (May 12, 2005), pp. 25 161- 25405.

[41] Clean Air Markets Group v. Pataki, 338 F.3d 82 (2d Cir. 2003).

[42] Clean Air Act Sec. 209.

[43] Clean Air Act Secs. 177 and 209.

[44] Clean Air Act Sec. 213 and 209(e).

[45] Clean Air Act Secs. 209(e) and 233.

[46] Clean Air Act Sec.21 1 (c) (4) (A). California is not prohibited from adopting fuel or fuel additive regulations. Clean Air Act Sec. 21 1(c)(4)(B). States may regulate for other purposes, as some have by adopting ethanol or biofuels mandates for purposes of improving local economies or energy security.

[47] Clean Air Act Sec. 21 1(c)(4)(C)(v). This largely limits State fuels to those already approved by EPA.

[48] See, e.g., letter from Committee on Energy and Commerce Committee Chairman Dingell and Vice Chair DeGette; Subcommittee Chairmen Boucher and Wynn; and Vice Chairs Butterfield and Solis to Appropriations Chairman Obey and Subcommittee Chairman Dicks (May 2, 2007), p. 2. Also see letter from then-Ranking Member Dingell and 61 other Members of the House to Appropriations Subcommittee Chairman Taylor and Ranking Member Dicks (April 28, 2006).

[49] These considerations should also be factors in determining what Federal programs are needed in addition to a capand-trade program

[50] For purposes of the initial discussion of the effect of different programs, it is assumed that States do not retire allowances equal to the reductions achieved by the program.

[51] This assumes that the reductions outside the cap are not used as offsets in the cap-and-trade program.

[52] "Retiring" allowances means that the State would take Federally-issued allowances that had not been used (or turned in to the Federal Government) and permanently take them out of circulation. Effectively, this action lowers the Federal cap. Theoretically, allowance retirements by States could be accomplished by allocating Federal allowances to States and authorizing them to retire allowances, or by authorizing States to require entities they regulate to turn in Federal allowances as part of the State program. The point of regulation in both the Federal and State program might affect whether the latter approach would be feasible and whether the State would be imposing an additional cost primarily on its own citizens or on citizens of other States. For example, if the Federal point of regulation is a stationary source that emits greenhouse gases, administrative burdens might not increase if a more stringent State program were to require that source to turn in extra allowances to the State. State allowance surrender requirements would seem to pose greater administrative burdens if the Federal point of regulation were upstream of the stationary source.

[53] This assumes that the reductions outside the cap are not used as offsets in the cap-and-trade program.

[54] See, e.g., Figure 2, Case C.

[55] Special transitional issues will be raised in the context of State cap-and-trade programs that will commence before a Federal program (e.g., RGGI is scheduled to start its first three-year compliance period in 2009).

[56] See, e.g., Figure 2, Case E.

[57] Committee on State Practices in Setting Mobile Source Emissions Standards, National Research Council, "State and Federal Standards for Mobile-Source Emissions" (2006), pp. 3-4.

[58] Funding might be through existing grant programs such as the Energy and Environment Block Grant (EEBG) program that was included in last year's energy bill (Energy Independence and Security Act of 2007, Section 544). The new energy law authorized $10 billion in grants to cities, counties, and States to help address climate change at the local level. Another possibility contained in S. 2191 would be to provide allowances (or allowance revenue) to States, which will be discussed in an upcoming white paper.

[59] National Assessment Synthesis Team, U.S. Global Change Research Program Climate Change Impacts on the United States; The Potential Consequences of Climate Variability and Change: Overview Report (2000), p. 7, http://www.usgcrp.gov/usgcrp /Library/nationalassessment /1IntroA. pdf.

[60] Due to a decision by EPA, the States cannot yet enforce these greenhouse gas tailpipe standards. Letter from EPA Administrator Johnson, opera cit.

[61] The domestic auto industry has expressed concern that it will be disproportionately and negatively affected by California's standards as compared to international auto companies.

[62] California Air Resources Board, "Clean Air Act Section 209(b) Request; California's Motor Vehicle Regulations to Control Greenhouse Gas Emissions" (December 21, 2005), Attachment 2 – Support Document, p. 18, http://www.regulations.gov/fdmspublic/component/main?main=Document Detail&d=EPA-HQ-OAR-2006-0173- 0004.1.

[63] The Committee is not considering changing the current process under the Clean Air Act Section 209(b) for State regulation of criteria and hazardous air pollutants; local emissions of these pollutants can cause local health and environmental problems. This circumstance stands in contrast to greenhouse gases, where climate change problems are due to global rather than local concentrations.

[64] This reluctance will be particularly evident in States that are developing cap-and-trade programs that would provide a revenue stream to the State from the sale or auction of allowances

[65] Domestic Automobile Industry is defined as General Motors, Ford Motor Company, and Chrysler LLC. States that have adopted or announced they will adopt CA greenhouse gas vehicle standards are as follows: AZ, CA, CO, CT, FL, ME, MD, MA, NJ, NM, NY, OR, PA, RI, UT, VT, and WA. Manufacturing jobs data from Memorandum from Shane Karr, Vice President of Federal Affairs, Alliance of Automobile Manufacturers, to Jonathan Brater, Committee on Energy and Commerce staff.

In: Constructing Climate Change Legislation...   ISBN 978-1-60692-986-5
Editor: Gerald P. Overhauser   © 2009 Nova Science Publishers, Inc.

Chapter 3

CLIMATE CHANGE LEGISLATION DESIGN WHITE PAPER COMPETITIVENESS CONCERNS/ENGAGING DEVELOPING COUNTRIES*

Committee on Energy and Commerce

The Committee on Energy and Commerce and its Subcommittee on Energy and Air Quality are issuing a series of Climate Change Legislation Design White Papers as the next step toward enactment of a mandatory, economy-wide climate change program. While the hearings earlier in this Congress were designed to give the Committee an understanding of the status and projected path of climate change and potential ways to address it, these White Papers and the hearings on them will focus on the construction of mandatory, economy-wide climate change legislation. The White Papers will describe the basic design and key principles of a regulatory program and also identify issues about which further information and discussion is desirable.

The first White Paper identified the economic sectors and activities that are directly emitting greenhouse gases (GHGs) and how those emissions could be included in a cap-andtrade program. This chapter discusses potential domestic

---

* This is an edited, excerpted and augmented edition of a Committee on Energy and Commerce Staff, dated January 2008.

legislative provisions that could encourage developing countries to curb their emissions of greenhouse gases.

EXECUTIVE SUMMARY

Under the 1992 United Nations Framework Convention on Climate Change (UNFCCC), both developed and developing country signatories recognized the need to limit emissions of greenhouse gases and to negotiate subsequent agreements to implement the treaty's common objectives. The procedural "roadmap" agreed to under the December 2007 "Bali Action Plan" aims to conclude an agreement by the end of 2009 that would specify emissions obligations for both developed and developing nations beginning in 2013 upon the expiration of the Kyoto Protocol. It is our intention to enact legislation to limit U.S. emissions prior to the time such an international agreement is adopted and enters into force. As we determine the components of a climate change program to which our Nation will commit, it is essential that the bill include incentives for developing nations such as China and India to curb their emissions for several reasons:

- First, limiting greenhouse gas emissions of the U.S. and other developed countries will not prevent dangerous interference with the climate system unless key developing countries also control their GHG emissions.
- Second, if the U.S. were to cap its own GHG emissions without corresponding action by developing nations that compete in global trade markets, the cost of producing some American products would increase relative to those manufactured in countries without emissions limits. As a result, U.S. industry and jobs might relocate to (or expand operations in) countries that do not limit the emissions of their industries, causing both the environment and the U.S. economy to suffer.
- Third, while there is precedent in international agreements for adopting differing obligations for developed and developing countries, past action on climate change suggests that Congress would be unlikely to adopt legislation committing the U.S. to reduce its GHG emission limits without action by developing countries as well.

Therefore, in contrast to international negotiations, consideration of domestic legislation does not involve all the parties whose actions contribute to the global problem of climate change. Since the U.S. cannot unilaterally bind other countries, our goal will be to craft legislation limiting U.S. carbon emissions that also induces developing countries to limit their emissions growth (1) on a timetable that meets both environmental and trade competitiveness concerns; (2) in a manner that is reasonably certain to withstand challenge before the World Trade Organization (WTO); and (3) on terms that pose acceptable risks to U.S. interests in the event of a negative WTO determination.

RATE OF GROWTH IN CARBON EMISSIONS OF DEVELOPING COUNTRIES

Climate change is affected by the volume of greenhouse gases emitted into the atmosphere over many years, without regard to the country in which the emissions occur. As a result, unlike most of this country's other environmental programs, a climate change program must take into account other countries' emissions and actions. It will take concerted action by the United States and other major emitting countries to prevent dangerous interference with the climate system.

A relatively small number of countries are responsible for most of the world's greenhouse gas emissions. The U.S., the EU-25, China, Russia, India, and Japan accounted for more than 60 percent of global greenhouse gas emissions in 2000. Adding in the next 9 highest emitting countries brings the total to 80 percent. See Figure 1.[1]

The sources of greenhouse gas emissions vary by country, as illustrated in Figure 2 for selected countries. According to testimony presented to the Subcommittee last year, land use changes were responsible for more than 60 percent of Brazil's 2000 emissions, but were a net emissions sink (i.e., reduced emissions) in some other countries. Agriculture was responsible for approximately 35 percent of India's emissions and 20 percent of Brazil's and China's emissions, but less than 10 percent of the emissions of the EU-25 and the United States. Energy accounted for more than 90 percent of U.S. emissions, more than 70 percent of the EU-25's and China's emissions, almost 60 percent of India's emissions, but less than 15 percent of Brazil's emissions.

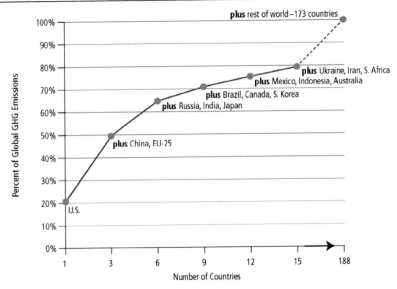

Source: Testimony of Dr. Jonathan Pershing, Director, Climate Energy and Pollution Program, World Resources Institute, before the Subcommittee on Energy and Air Quality on March 27, 2007, (p. 17)

Figure 1. Major Emitting Countries' Contributions to Greenhouse Gas Emissions (2000 Data, 6 Gases).

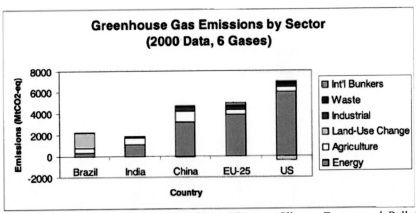

Source: Testimony of Dr. Jonathan Pershing, Director, Climate Energy and Pollution Program, World Resources Institute, before the Subcommittee on Energy and Air Quality on March 27, 2007, p. 14.

Figure 2. Greenhouse Gas Emissions by Sector (2000 Data, 6 Gases).

Business-as-usual projections indicate there will be some significant changes in these comparative emissions data. The International Energy Agency (IEA) issued a 2007 report projecting that global energy demand would increase by more than one-half by 2030, and that "Developing countries..contribute 74 percent of the increase in global primary energy use.. China and India alone account for 45 percent of this increase."[2] The IEA also predicted that fossil fuels will remain the dominant source of energy, and that coal would account for the biggest increase in demand in absolute terms, primarily due to power generation.[3]

This report made headlines for its prediction that worldwide energy-related carbon-dioxide emissions will increase 57 percent between 2005 and 2030 (an 1.8 percent annual increase).[4] It projected that developing countries will account for more than three-quarters of the increase in global CO_2 emissions between 2005 and 2030, and that these countries' overall share in world emissions would rise from 40 percent in 2005 to nearly 55 percent by 2030.[5]

The most striking estimates had to do with increased carbon dioxide emissions from China:

China and India together account for 56% of the increase in emissions between 2005 and 2030. China is by far the biggest single contributor to incremental emissions [and] is expected to overtake the United States in 2007 as the world's biggest emitter. One reason for the strong increase in China's emissions is the significant quantity of fossil energy and, therefore, carbon embodied in the goods that China produces for export, which far outweighs the carbon embodied in its imports.[6]

The projected large increase in China's emissions continues to draw widespread notice. A report by the Pew Center on Global Climate Change noted that "China is the world's second largest greenhouse gas emitter after the United States and its emissions are increasing rapidly with strong economic growth and rising energy demand."[7] The report continued "China's emissions are projected to continue rising rapidly — another 65% to 80% by 2020 - and annual emissions may surpass those of the United States as early as 2009."[8]

Figure 3 shows similar data from a 2007 Energy Information Administration report projecting increased energy-related carbon dioxide emissions from China and the U.S., as well as India and other countries.[9]

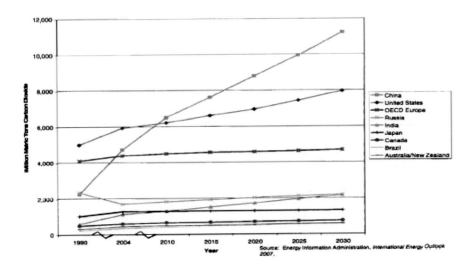

Figure 3. Projected Carbon Dioxide Emissions (Energy-Related) for Select Countries.

Concern about emissions in the major developing countries arises not only from their growth and magnitude, but also from the concern that a stringent limit on U S emissions could contribute to a shift in economic activity (and corresponding greenhouse gas emissions) from the United States to a country without any greenhouse gas limitations.

U.N. FRAMEWORK CONVENTION ON CLIMATE CHANGE, KYOTO PROTOCOL, RECENT DEVELOPMENTS

Due to the global nature of climate change and the need for global action, climate change has been the subject of international discussions and negotiations for many years. The primary objective of the 1992 UNFCCC was "stabilization of greenhouse gas concentrations in the atmosphere at a level that would prevent dangerous anthropogenic interference with the climate system." The 1992 Treaty applies to both developed and developing nations and commits both groups to "common but differentiated responsibilities" for reducing greenhouse gas emissions. The 1992 Treaty states that developed nations should take the lead in mitigating climate change, with a goal of reducing and stabilizing emissions at 1990 levels by the year 2000.[10]

In 1997, the UNFCCC negotiations produced the Kyoto Protocol, [11] which established binding emissions reduction targets for developed countries during the first "budget period" of 2008-2012, with an overall goal of reducing industrialized countries' total emissions by at least 5 percent below their 1990 levels over that time period.[12]

Although the U.S. signed the Kyoto Protocol in 1998, President Clinton did not submit it to the Senate for approval, reflecting the political reality signaled by the Senate's unanimous passage in 1997 of S. Res. 98, the Byrd-Hagel resolution. This resolution stated that no treaty mandating commitments for developed countries should be ratified unless it also requires developing countries to reduce their emissions within the same compliance period. In 2001, the Administration of President George W. Bush formally rejected the Protocol.

Annual "Conferences of the Parties" (COPs) to the 1992 Treaty continue, with the U.S. participating in discussions under the Treaty, but not those specific to the Kyoto Protocol. Progress on potential post-2012 "next steps" has been inconclusive, and the COPs in Montreal (2005) and Nairobi (2006) produced no clear path forward. Expectations for the December 2007 COP in Bali were modest, and discussions leading to the "Bali Action Plan" were very contentious. The outcome, however, was generally viewed as positive, and "participants generally lauded the final agreement as one that sets a negotiating framework in place, and includes developed and developing countries in the negotiations on 'considerations' for a final agreement.. ."[13]

In 2005, the Bush Administration initiated a voluntary program on a "parallel track" to the U.N. process, the "Asia-Pacific Partnership for Clean Development and Climate." This initiative includes several significant developing countries (China, India, and South Korea), as well as developed countries that signed the Protocol (Japan) and developed Nations that did not sign the Protocol (the U.S. and Australia). In September 2007, President Bush held a climate change summit in Washington, D.C. (the "Major Economies Meeting on Energy Security and Climate Change") to which he invited ministers from eight major developed countries and seven of the largest developing countries. President Bush's proposal that GHG emissions should be addressed through adoption of voluntary long-term goals drew mixed reaction.[14] A second "Major Economies" meeting is scheduled for late January in Honolulu.

POLICY OPTIONS FOR ENCOURAGING DEVELOPING NATIONS TO LIMIT THEIR CARBON EMISSIONS

Legislation establishing a domestic program to limit U.S. emissions of greenhouse gases should include incentives for developing nations to curb their emissions, particularly in the absence of an international agreement establishing mandatory emission reduction obligations for all major emitting countries. On the environmental side, such an approach would have the advantage of committing the U.S. to lessen its contribution to the problem of global climate change, and simultaneously encouraging developing countries to do the same. From an economic viewpoint, such an approach could mitigate the risk that, in the absence of significant developing country commitments, unilateral action by the U.S. could harm the competitiveness of our industries in world markets and result in the loss of American jobs.[15]

Many factors will affect each country's willingness to curb its greenhouse gas emissions.[16] This paper is not intended to be a discussion of all the factors affecting these decisions. Rather, it focuses on the narrower issue of how to use domestic legislation to provide additional reasons for other countries to curb greenhouse gas emissions.

A fundamental question in structuring legislation is whether the U.S. must "go first" before developing countries will agree to limit their own greenhouse gas emissions. Some observers believe that developing nations view a prior U.S. commitment to reduce its GHG emissions as an absolute prerequisite to limiting their own emissions, and that in the near term their paramount focus will be on economic growth.[17]

As an alternative, a number of commenters have suggested the U.S. might adopt a hybrid approach that uses trade policy as a tool, and one witness before the Subcommittee on Energy and Air Quality suggested that "Congress can design the U.S. carbon market to provide carrots and sticks that encourage other countries — even recalcitrant ones — to join our efforts."[18]

Others have argued, however, that any U.S. legislation that is perceived as heavy handed by developing countries could have drawbacks. In particular, it has been suggested that while conditioning U.S. action on that of developing countries might spur the latter to action, it could also backfire and have the opposite effect.[19]

Accordingly, the debate about developing country incentives involves both timing questions (must the U.S. limit its emissions in advance of any expectation or requirement that developing countries do the same?) and determinations of which approach would be most likely to stimulate developing countries to limit their GHG emissions (carrots, sticks, or both?).

In addition, there is considerable disagreement as to what approach would be most likely to pass muster with the World Trade Organization (WTO), and resulting concern about the effect on U.S. industry should a challenge be successful. That effect is particularly difficult to predict since, as one scholar observed, "Any competitiveness provision with a serious trade impact is likely to trigger a WTO complaint" and that "Given the vague nature of WTO law.. [it] may either uphold or strike down the provision."[20]

Because this paper's focus is on legislative options to encourage developing countries to curb their greenhouse gas emissions, it does not address the role of technology development and deployment in reducing their greenhouse gas emissions. Affordable technology will be one key factor in the willingness of developing countries to curb their greenhouse gas emissions. A

domestic U.S. program that spurs such developments should have the double benefit of aiding the environment and accelerating U.S. industrial development in emerging low GHG emitting technologies.[21]

The following discussion outlines three legislative approaches that have been suggested to ensure that developing countries curb their emissions, so that the environmental objectives of climate change legislation can be achieved and the competitiveness of American industry is not adversely affected.[22] These approaches fall into three broad categories:

1   Border Adjustments — trade-related policies that use tariffs, taxes, or other mechanisms such as requiring foreign goods imported into the U.S. to be accompanied by emissions allowances;

2   Performance Standards — a "non-market-based" type of regulation, such as emission standards or carbon intensity-based regulations; and

3   Carbon Market Design — imposing conditions for other countries' access to and participation in the U.S. carbon market established in a climate change bill.

International Brotherhood of Electrical Workers-American Electric Power IBEW/AEP Proposal — Many elements of this approach, which was announced in February 2007, were later incorporated into S. 1766 (introduced by Senators Bingaman and Specter) and S. 2191 (introduced by Senators Lieberman and Warner and reported last year by the Senate Committee on Environment and Public Works). The proposal requires that, in order to import certain "greenhouse gas intensive goods" into the U.S., the importer must submit allowances to cover the emissions produced during the manufacturing process. Failure to submit allowances would bar the entry of such goods into the United States.

The requirement would apply to "greenhouse gas intensive goods" from countries that the President determines have not taken "comparable action," as compared to the U.S., to reduce their emissions. The requirement would apply only to countries described as "large emitters" of GHG emissions, and would exempt goods from a "least developed country" or one with "de minimis" emission levels. "Greenhouse gas intensive goods" would include those produced by the iron and steel, aluminum, cement, bulk glass, and paper industries.

The allowance submission requirement would first apply several years after the effective date of a U.S. cap-and-trade program began.[23] During the interim, the U.S. would have to make "good faith efforts" to persuade foreign countries to limit their GHG emissions. The application of allowance submission requirements to goods from a specific country would be triggered only in the event of its failure to negotiate a GHG agreement with the U.S., and upon a Presidential

determination that the country is not taking "comparable action" to limit its emissions. The unilateral imposition by the U.S. of such trade requirements is described by the sponsors as a measure of "last resort."

The IBEW/AEP proposal background material states that "major emitting nations would likely join a climate regime and reduce their GHG emissions rather than buy large numbers of allowances.."[24] It further asserts that this approach "respects WTO ground-rules" and that "in anticipation of a cap and trade regulatory system the IBEW/AEP allowance requirement has been specifically designed to be consistent with the WTO and ensure international action."[25]

At this point, there appears to be no consensus as to whether the IBEW/AEP "border adjustment" proposal would fully protect U.S. competitiveness, or whether it would survive a potential challenge with respect to WTO rules. On the positive side, one article observed that "In the best case, a policy of border adjustments will effectively protect vulnerable domestic firms or industries against adverse competitiveness impacts from a domestic climate policy while simultaneously creating incentives for other nations to reduce their emissions." The author, however, notes that to satisfy WTO standards "great sensitivity must be shown..including the need to put major trade partners on notice and provide sufficient time for them to develop viable domestic emissions reduction policies."[26]

A legal treatise on the subject suggested that, if structured properly, such a border adjustment policy might be upheld either as consistent with General Agreement on Tariffs and Trade (GATT) rules[27] or, alternatively, under the environmental exceptions in GATT Article XX.[28] Nonetheless, the author notes that the "WTO consistency of such process-based restrictions is unclear and remains to be tested."[29]

Nonetheless, the IBEW/AEP approach has been criticized by some as vulnerable under WTO rules, and in any event as providing incomplete protection for U.S. industry. A September 25, 2007, letter from the Industrial Energy Consumers of America (IECA) to various Members of Congress argues that the proposal will not assure a level playing field between U.S. produced energy intensive products and those that are imported, because of the time gap between the date when greenhouse gas caps would apply to U.S. domestic industry and the date when emission allowances would be required of foreign competitors.[30]

Similarly, a recent memorandum from the American Iron and Steel Institute (AISI) cited the possibility that foreign governments might subsidize their industries' compliance costs, and argued the proposal faces "a substantial risk of violating international law."[31]

Performance Standards/Regulations on Imports of Carbon Intensive Products — An alternative to the "border adjustment" approach is to include in climate legislation a requirement for the establishment of "carbon intensity standards" that would apply to all energy intensive materials sold in U.S. commerce, whether of foreign or domestic origin. Industries often cited as "energy intensive" (and thus vulnerable should adoption of a GHG emissions caps increase energy prices) include cement, steel, and glass.[32]

Such a performance standard could be established either by Congress or under authority delegated to an executive branch agency, and would set a per ton (or other unit) limit on the amount of carbon that could be emitted during production (whether the item is manufactured in the U.S. or abroad). One frequently discussed option, a "carbon intensity cap," could involve differing standards for different technologies or manufacturing processes, and the implementing agency could be directed to adjust it downwards over time to a "lowest achievable" standard.

For the relevant U.S. industries, one question is whether such a regulatory regime would be separate from, or in addition to, obligations under a domestic cap and trade regime. Under some proposals, manufacturers would be exempt from allowance requirements under a U.S. domestic cap and trade system, since their costs likely would be affected by higher energy prices for purchases from entities that are subject to emissions caps (e.g. electric utilities or natural gas producers).

As in the case of the IBEW/AEP border adjustment proposal, it does not appear at present that a consensus exists with respect to either the policy merits of a carbon intensity performance standard approach or its conformance with WTO rules.

One discussion of such an approach notes that "well-crafted performance standards have the potential to encourage efficiency improvements without putting as much upward pressure on domestic production costs" as market-based policies, and as a result "may seem less likely..to raise competitiveness concerns for industries that face international competition and to create incentives for shifting production abroad."[33]

On the other hand, the same author suggests that "Identifying the specific industries that are most likely to be adversely affected by a mandatory domestic GHG-reduction policy is complex.."[34] and that as a general rule performance standards "are more costly than broad market-based approaches because they do not encourage end users to reduce their consumption of GHG-intensive goods."[35]

Moreover, one of the reservations leveled at carbon tax proposals — that they do not provide certainty with respect to the total amount of carbon reductions to be achieved — may also be leveled against some proposals for performance standards. Although performance standards place a limit on the per unit carbon intensity during manufacturing, they do not limit the amount that can be produced and hence do not impose finite domestic or international emissions caps.

In terms of such an approach's legality under WTO rules, it has been suggested that a carbon intensity performance standard might successfully be defended as an "environmental standard" as defined by the Agreement on Technical Barriers to Trade (TBT). [36] Adoption of this approach might not require as lengthy a period of negotiation as would be required before imposition of a "border adjustment," and Congress could delegate authority to set and adjust such standards over time to reflect technology improvements.

As in the case of a trade tool, questions have been raised about the likelihood that a performance standard would survive legal challenge before the WTO, and questions have been raised as to whether prior WTO holdings suggest that TBT rules would support imposition of a carbon intensity standard.[37] The TBT Agreement also may require differing standards for developing countries if "full application would not be compatible with developing country Members' development, financial and trade needs."[38]

Environmental Defense "Carrots and Sticks" Proposal to Impose Conditions on Access to U.S. Carbon Markets — Under this approach, in establishing a U.S. carbon market, Congress would stipulate conditions that will encourage developing nations to limit their emissions. In testimony before the Subcommittee on Energy and Air Quality, Environmental Defense (ED) proposed a number of specific "carrot and stick" options to this end, noting that fast-growing, developing countries will soon have higher emissions than the U.S. and thus

"Global warming can't be solved unless both the U.S. and large developing countries cut total GHG emissions."[39]

While urging that Congress give careful consideration to a border adjustment approach such as the IBEW/AEP proposal, ED also outlined a number of provisions Congress could include in establishing a cap-and-trade market to provide incentives for developing countries to act, noting that "our carbon market is likely to be the largest in the world.. [and] Other nations will want access to our market — for carbon finance, and to sell us credits." ED encouraged Congress to consider incorporating in legislation the following types of "carrots and sticks" in designing a carbon market:

- Offer emission "premiums" for countries that sign up to emission caps early. Congress could offer carbon market access on more generous terms to nations that sign up early for emissions caps, and perhaps offer them more lenient cap-and-trade targets;
- Levy mandatory "multipliers" on emission credits generated in uncapped countries. For nations that haven't capped their emissions, Congress could impose conditions on their sale of credits to U.S. emitters that require more than a one-for-one ratio, thus strengthening their incentive to reduce their own emissions;
- Instruct the Executive Branch to negotiate carbon market access agreements with other countries.[40]

THE WORLD TRADE ORGANIZATION — PROCESS FOR RESOLUTION OF TRADE DISPUTES

Any provisions inducing developing countries to limit greenhouse gas emissions will have to pass muster before the World Trade Organization (WTO). The WTO is the primary international organization governing world trade,[41] and administers agreements covering goods and services in international commerce that apply to "virtually all government practices that directly relate to trade",[42] including tariffs and subsidies.

WTO agreements are founded on the principles of nondiscriminatory treatment among countries, negotiated limits on trade barriers, and agreement to settle disputes under specified procedures with a range of remedies. Decisions about WTO rules and procedures, including settlement of trade disputes, are made by the member countries. [43] Since 1994, the WTO has administered a dispute resolution system with a binding process for settling disagreements through the Dispute Settlement Body (DSB).[44]

Under this process, the first step is consultation between the governments of the countries involved, and if this fails, the complainant may ask the DSB to convene a dispute panel to hear the case. If a complaint is upheld, the prevailing party may either seek to negotiate a compensation agreement or re9uest the DSB to suspend normal trade obligations and permit it to impose a retaliatory measure.[45]

Importantly, where retaliatory measures are in order, the complaining country may, in some circumstances, impose a countermeasure in a sector other than that involved in the specific dispute until the offending measure is ended or the parties reach another resolution.[46]

While aspects of the WTO regime are controversial, and there is an ongoing debate within Congress about the costs and benefits of U.S. membership, so long as the U.S. remains a member it is bound by that body's dispute resolution mechanisms.

POTENTIAL IMPLICATIONS OF WTO RULES/PROCESS FOR U.S. CLIMATE CHANGE LEGISLATION

While at present there is no legislative consensus on developing countries policy, there is a general expectation that a WTO challenge is likely regardless of what approach Congress takes.

If such a challenge to the trade provisions of a climate law were upheld, the U.S. could face difficult choices such as whether to negotiate a settlement or face retaliation by the prevailing country. As one scholar observed, if a U.S. climate law were found to violate WTO law "the only remedy currently offered by the WTO dispute settlement system is that the United States would then have to change its legislation as to the future (or suffer retaliation if it fails to do so..)".[47]

The key point is that while Congress has control over which trade-related measure to include in a climate bill, the determination of such a provision's legitimacy under WTO rules is out of U.S. hands. There is a risk that the bill's domestic provisions binding U.S. industry could take effect during an initial time period, and related provisions aimed at our trade competitors' behavior ultimately could be determined to violate WTO rules. In that event, the intended linkage between U.S. carbon limits and the conduct of major emitting countries with whom we compete would be broken, unless Congress halted implementation of the domestic program. Not only could U.S. industry be disadvantaged in terms of its international competitiveness, but the bill's fundamental environmental purpose could be defeated. In a worst case scenario, emissions from our trading partners could increase, the environmental benefit of any U.S reductions could be overwhelmed by emissions growth elsewhere, domestic industry could be harmed and jobs lost, and U.S. industry could face unpredictable retaliatory measures as a result of a negative WTO determination.

Questions for Further Discussion

1   Do any of the three alternatives discussed in this chapter - border adjustments, performance standards, or carbon market design - offer clear cut advantages as a legislative policy in terms of encouraging developing countries to limit their GHG emissions and simultaneously protecting U.S. industry in global trade markets? Are there other approaches Congress should consider and, if so, what are their advantages and disadvantages?

2   Are the various policies mutually exclusive, or can they be combined in some fashion to achieve the best balance between reducing global GHG emissions and protecting U.S. industry and jobs?

3   In terms of timing, how closely should legislation link commencement of a U.S. domestic cap-and—trade regime with policies to induce developing countries to limit their GHG emissions?

4   Should U.S. legislation distinguish between the "least developed" countries and other "developing" countries?

5   Which approach is most likely to satisfy WTO requirements? Which approach is most likely to result in the prompt resolution of any WTO challenge, and thereby provide more certainty with respect to both global environmental benefits and the long term impact on U.S. industry and jobs?

How can climate legislation that includes both domestic and international components be drafted to align with any post-Kyoto Protocol accord the U.S. agrees to under the UNFCCC? How might U.S. adoption of climate change legislation affect the likelihood that such an agreement is concluded and influence the formulation of a U.S. international negotiating position?

APPENDIX A: COMPARISON OF COUNTRIES' GREENHOUSE GAS EMISSIONS

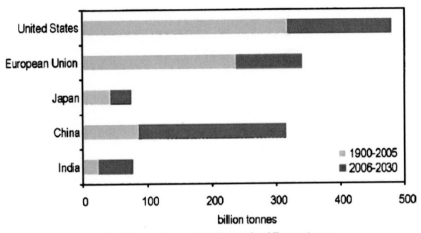

Source: *World Energy Outlook 2007*, International Energy Agency.

Source: *World Energy Outlook 2007,* International Energy Agency.

Figure 4. Cumulative Energy-Related CO2 Emissions for Select Countries, 1900-2030.

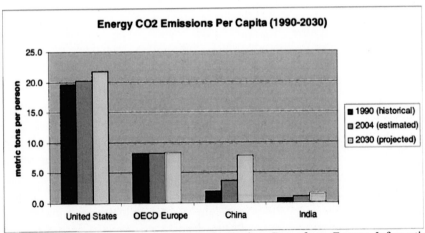

Source: Graph from Congressional Research Service; Data from Energy Information Administration, International Energy Outlook 2007.

Figure 5. Energy CO2 emissions per capita (1990-2030).

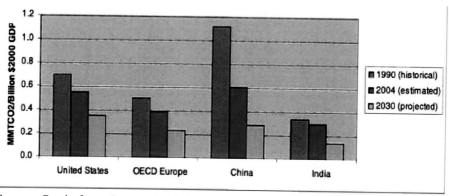

Source: Graph from Congressional Research Service; Data from Energy Information Administration, International Energy Outlook 2007. MIVITCO2 is million metric tons of carbon dioxide.

Figure 6. Energy CO2 Emissions Intensity (1990-2030).

REFERENCES

[1] There are other informative ways to compare emissions from different countries. Appendix A contains three graphs that compare select countries' cumulative greenhouse gas emissions from 1900 to 2030, per capita emissions, and per gross domestic product emissions.

[2] World Energy Outlook 2007, International Energy Agency, p. 42.

[3] Id. at 54.

[4] Id. at 192.

[5] Ibid at 199.

[6] Ibid at 196.

[7] "Climate Change Mitigation Measures in the People's Republic of China," April 2007, Pew Center on Global Climate Change," p. 1.

[8] Ibid.

[9] International Energy Outlook 2007, Energy Information Administration (EIA).

[10] The Treaty, sometimes referred to as the Rio Treaty, was ratified by the U.S. during the Administration of President George H. W. Bush and went "into force" in 1994.

[11] The Protocol went into force in 2005 and, according to a UNFCCC report, had been ratified or accepted by 168 nations and the European Union by the end of 2006.

[12] The Protocol adopted legally binding, mandatory emissions reductions targets for the six major greenhouse gases, of which the most "prominent" and "most pervasive in human activity" is carbon dioxide. Congressional Research Service (CRS), "Climate Change: the Kyoto Protocol and International Actions," August 22, 2007, p. 2.

[13] "Climate Change Negotiations: The Bali Action Plan," Congressional Research Service, January 11, 2008, p. 2.

[14] "Bush's Alternative to Kyoto Pact on Warming Gets a Cool Response." Wall Street Journal, September 30, 2007, A5.

[15] At a March 27, 2007, hearing of the Subcommittee on Energy and Air Quality, Boise Cascade LLC testified "This is clearly a global issue and environmental practices in other parts of the world have a clear and direct impact on the U.S. and its citizens..if we do not hold our developing trading partners to the same standards, we will ship both the jobs and the greenhouse gas production overseas." Testimony of W. Thomas Stephens, Chairman and Chief Executive Officer, p. 8.

[16] For example, according to testimony presented to the Subcommittee, China's desire to improve its energy security could provide an incentive for it to adopt measures that also reduce greenhouse gas emissions. See testimony of Dr. Jonathan Pershing, Director, Climate Energy and Pollution Program, World Resources Institute, before the Subcommittee on Energy and Air Quality on March 27, 2007.

[17] See testimony of Mr. Pramit Pal Chaudhuri, New York and Foreign Editor, Hindustan Times, before the Subcommittee on Energy and Air Quality on March 27, 2007.

[18] March 27, 2007, testimony of Annie Petsonk, International Counsel, Environmental Defense, p. 10. Ms. Petsonk further stated that "most developing countries are reluctant to take further climate protection steps unless and until the United States does.. [and are] not likely to take more stringent or faster steps than the US does."

[19] The Pew Center has stated that "Making future U.S. action expressly contingent on the efforts of other countries may provide some further inducement for action. Alternatively, by appearing irresolute, it may deter others from commencing ambitious long-term effort" (www.pewclimate.org/policy_center/analyses/sec/q4.cfm.) Similarly, one legal scholar observed that "Competitiveness provisions, and the unilateral action that comes with them, may undermine the trust necessary for future international cooperation and agreement on emission reductions. This is the potential flip-side of one of the hoped for benefits of a competitiveness

provision." (Working Paper "U.S. Federal Climate Policy and Competitiveness Concerns: The Limits and Options of International Trade Law," Joost Pauwelyn, Nicholas Institute for Environmental Policy Solutions, Duke University, p 6.)

[20] "U.S. Federal Climate Policy and Competitiveness Concerns: The Limits and Options of International Trade Law," Joost Pauwelyn, Nicholas, Institute for Environmental Policy Solutions, Duke University, p. 7.

[21] This is what is reported to have occurred from implementation of the Montreal Protocol. The Montreal Protocol, which requires the phase-out of chemicals that cause damage to the stratospheric ozone layer, required developed countries to comply long before developing countries had to comply. Not only has the Montreal Protocol been successful in moving towards repair of the hole in the ozone layer, but EPA reports that U.S. companies that developed substitute chemicals for our country were then able to export those chemicals to developing countries.

[22] Competitiveness issues for some industries might also be addressed through the distribution of allowances, which will be discussed in a later White Paper.

[23] The most recent iteration of the IBEW/AEP proposal estimates the period between the imposition of allowance requirements applying to U.S. producers, and allowance requirements applying to U.S. imports of covered goods, as roughly three years. Under S. 1766 and S. 2191, a longer period of 8 years would apply.

[24] ibid.

[25] Ibid.

[26] Morgenstern, Richard. "Addressing Competitiveness Concerns in the Context of a Mandatory Policy for Reducing U.S. Greenhouse Gas Emissions," Assessing U.S. Climate Policy Options; A report summarizing work at RFF as part of the inter-industry U.S. Climate Policy Forum. Resources for the Future, November 2007, p. 116.

[27] Pauwelyn, op. cit., 3.

[28] Thid p. 3.

[29] Ibid. p. 41.

[30] Industrial Energy Consumers of America (IECA), September 25, 2007, letter to Senators Boxer and Inhofe and Representatives Dingell and Barton.

[31] "Climate Change, a Global Problem Requiring a Global Solution," American Iron and Steel Institute.

[32] The IECA letter also identifies as "energy intensive" the plastics, paper, food processing, aluminum, chemical, fertilizer, brick, insulation, industrial

gases, pharmaceutical, construction products, automotive products, and brewing industries.

[33] Morgenstern p. 113.

[34] Id at p. 116.

[35] Id. at p. 113.

[36] The TBT Agreement is an integral part of the WTO Agreement concerning countries' technical regulations and standards that specify a product's technical characteristics or production process. For a description of the TBT program, see "Technical Barriers to Trade" at www.wto.org.

[37] Pauwleyn op. cit., p. 27.

[38] "Technical Information on Technical Barriers to Trade," www.wto.org, p. 8.

[39] Petsonk, op. cit., p. 2.

[40] Id. at 10-13.

[41] The WTO in 1995 succeeded the General Agreement on Tariffs and Trade (GATT), which went into effect in 1948. The WTO is located in Geneva Switzerland, and includes 150 members and 31 observer governments representing more 95 percent of world trade. www.wto.org.

[42] CRS, "The World Trade Organization: Background and Issues," summary.

[43] www.vvto.org.

[44] CRS observes that although the WTO "cannot force members to adhere to their obligations," as a member the U.S. has committed to follow its rules, which require that "Each Member shall ensure the conformity of its laws, regulations and administrative procedures with its obligations as provided in the annexed Agreements." Id. at 6.

[45] A determination that a U.S. measure violates a WTO agreement does not have "direct legal effect" in this country, and indeed Federal law is not affected unless Congress or the Executive Branch modifies the relevant law or administrative policy. CRS, "Dispute Settlement in the World Trade Organization: An Overview," p. 5.

[46] For example, in a long-running dispute over the banana regime in which the DSB upheld a U.S. complaint, the U.S. imposed tariffs on a list of eight items, including "bath preparations." U.S. imports of these products from the United Kingdom dropped 83 percent (and French imports dropped 45 percent) within 4 quarters. CRS, "Trade Retaliation: The 'Carousel' Approach," pp. 2-3.

[47] Pauwleyn, p. 7.

In: Constructing Climate Change Legislation...   ISBN 978-1-60692-986-5
Editor: Gerald P. Overhauser   © 2009 Nova Science Publishers, Inc.

Chapter 4

CLIMATE CHANGE LEGISLATION DESIGN WHITE PAPER SCOPE OF A CAP-AND-TRADE PROGRAM*

Committee on Energy and Commerce

The Committee on Energy and Commerce and its Subcommittee on Energy and Air Quality are issuing a series of Climate Change Legislation Design White Papers as the next step in the legislative process leading to enactment of a mandatory, economy-wide climate change program. While the hearings earlier in the year were designed to give the Committee an understanding of the status and projected path of climate change and potential ways to address it, these White Papers and the hearings on them will focus the Committee's attention on crafting mandatory, economy-wide climate change legislation. The White Papers will lay out the basic design and key principles of a program, and also identify issues about which further information and discussion is needed.

This chapter addresses the scope and coverage of the climate change program. It discusses what sectors and activities are directly emitting greenhouse gases, and how those emissions could be included in a cap-and-trade program. Other White Papers will address a number of other cap-and-trade design elements and additional topics, including: cap levels and timetables, measures for containing costs in a cap-and-trade program, carbon sequestration, offsets and credits,

---

* This is an edited, excerpted and augmented edition of a Committee on Energy and Commerce Staff, dated October 2007

developing countries, distribution of allowances, and additional measures to complement the cap-and-trade program.

EXECUTIVE SUMMARY

Based on the hearings earlier this year, the Committee and Subcommittee Chairmen have reached the following conclusions: The United States should reduce its greenhouse gas emissions by between 60 and 80 percent by 2050 to contribute to global efforts to address climate change. To do so, the United States should adopt an economy-wide, mandatory greenhouse gas reduction program. The central component of this program should be a capand-trade program. Given the breadth of the economy that will be affected by a national climate change program and the significant environmental consequences at stake, it is important to design a fair program that obtains the maximum emission reductions at the lowest cost and with the least economic disruption. The Subcommittee and full Committee will draft legislation to establish such a program.

The program will cover the following greenhouse gases: carbon dioxide (84% of U.S. greenhouse gas emissions in 2005), methane (7%), nitrous oxide (7%) and fluorinated gases (2%). Carbon dioxide (CO2) comes largely from burning fossil fuels. Methane is from a variety of sources, including oil and gas systems, landfills, agricultural activities, coal mines, and wastewater treatment facilities. Nitrous oxide derives largely from agricultural practices. Fluorinated gases are used largely for refrigeration and air conditioning. Industrial processes also produce some greenhouse gases as by-products. The following economic sectors directly emit greenhouse gases: electricity generation (34% of U.S. greenhouse gas emissions), transportation (28%), industrial (19%), commercial (6%), residential (5%), and agricultural (8%).

The cap-and-trade program will have increasingly stringent caps on greenhouse gas emissions, eventually reaching a level that reduces emissions by 60 to 80 percent in 2050. The Government will distribute allowances equal to the level of allowed greenhouse gas emissions. Allowances can then be bought and sold. Compliance is demonstrated by having regulated entities turn in a sufficient number of allowances to cover emissions. At its core, a cap-andtrade program is a method of tracking and accounting for greenhouse gas emissions and having the cost of those emissions factored into economic decisions.

We start with a strong presumption that all greenhouse gas emissions from all sectors should be covered by the cap-and-trade program. This desire must, however, be balanced with the need to have a workable program. There are practical limits to the number and type of entities that can be directly regulated by a cap-and-trade program. Accurate reporting and monitoring are critical to the program's success. If emissions from certain activities cannot be measured accurately, it may not be possible to require a regulated entity to turn in allowances to cover those emissions. In addition, it is impractical to require allowances to be turned in by a very large number of sources that are each responsible for very low emissions; it would increase the complexity and transaction costs of the program to an unacceptable level.

Selecting the regulated entities, or setting the point of regulation (the parties responsible for tracking emissions and turning in allowances), is very different for a cap-and-trade program than it is for more traditional forms of regulation. Traditionally, the regulated entity is the source that emits the pollution because it is capable of installing controls to reduce its emissions. This could also be the point of regulation in a cap-and-trade program, as it is in the Acid Rain Trading Program, which requires electricity generators to monitor emissions and turn in allowances. Alternatively, for some sectors or some activities, it would be impractical (if not impossible) for the cap-and-trade program to have the sources that emit greenhouse gases be the point of regulation. This obstacle is perhaps most apparent in the transportation sector, where the sources that emit greenhouse gases are individual vehicles.

In a cap-and-trade program, the point of regulation could be set at one of various points along the stream of economic activity that results in greenhouse gas emissions. For example, since the carbon content of fuel is an accurate measure of the CO_2 emitted when the fuel is burned, refiners or importers could be the point of regulation for the transportation sector. As long as emissions are accounted for once, and only once, the point of regulation does not have to be the same for all sectors and types of emissions. This chapter explores the possible points of regulation for each sector.

Although the cap-and-trade program will be the central component of a national climate change program, other measures will also be necessary. The Committee Chairman has already indicated that tax policy could play an important role in reducing greenhouse gases.

Other possible measures include efficiency or other performance standards, incentives for the purchase of advanced technology, and funding for research, development, and deployment of advanced technology. Potential complementary measures will be explored more thoroughly later in this process.

KEY DESIGN PRINCIPLES

Earlier this year, the Subcommittee on Energy and Air Quality held a series of climate change hearings. Based on those hearings, the Committee and Subcommittee Chairmen have concluded that:

- The United States needs to reduce its greenhouse gas emissions by 60 to 80 percent by 2050 to contribute to global efforts to address climate change.
- The United States needs an economy-wide, mandatory greenhouse gas reduction program.
- The central component of this program will be a cap-and-trade program, although other measures will also be needed.

A consensus is developing that the United States should reduce its greenhouse gas emissions by 60 to 80 percent by 2050 to contribute to global efforts to stabilize long term atmospheric greenhouse gas concentrations at a CO_2 equivalent level between 450 to 550 parts per million.[1] At this concentration range, global average surface warming would be very unlikely to be less than 1.5 degrees centigrade according to the Intergovernmental Panel on Climate Change.[2]

The climate change program must be an economy-wide program that accounts for all greenhouse gas emissions in the United States because (1) dramatic emissions reductions are required, (2) many economic sectors contribute to greenhouse gas emissions, and (3) everyone must fairly share responsibility for reductions. An economy-wide climate change program does not mean, however, that all sectors contribute their fair share in the same way.

The cornerstone of the program will be a cap-and-trade program. One key benefit of a cap-and-trade program is that it provides certainty that the selected level of greenhouse gas reductions will occur. In contrast, performance standards generally limit the rate of emissions (such as by controlling the average amount of carbon in motor vehicle fuel), but would allow emissions to increase (such as would happen if motor vehicle fuel use increased). A carbon or gasoline tax would provide an economic incentive to decrease the use of carbon fuels and would provide certainty about the cost of the program. Although a tax could be set at a level expected to produce the desired emissions decrease, it could not guarantee it. Another benefit of a cap-and-trade program is that it provides economic incentives for industry to find the lowest cost method of achieving the desired emissions reductions, encouraging and rewarding innovation that might not otherwise occur under more traditional regulatory or government research programs.

Even with a broad-based cap-and-trade program, complementary measures (such as a carbon tax or other tax-based incentives, efficiency or other performance standards, or research and development programs) will also be needed. For example, funding for research, development, and deployment of new technologies would assist industries that will need to adopt new technologies. In addition, efficiency or other performance standards might be appropriate for some economic actors that would be inappropriate to include directly in a capand-trade program, but that should contribute to an economy-wide reduction program in some other way.[3]

COVERAGE -- GREENHOUSE GASES

The program will cover the following greenhouse gases:

- Carbon Dioxide (CO2),
- Methane (CH4),
- Nitrous Oxide (N20), and
- Fluorinated Gases: Hydrofluorocarbons (HFCs), Perfluorocarbons (PFCs), and Sulfur Hexafluoride (SF6).

Figure 1 shows the relevant contribution of each gas to the United States total greenhouse gas emissions.[4] CO2 emissions, largely the result of burning fossil fuels, are the biggest share (84%) of U.S. emissions. The two largest sources of methane emissions are oil and gas systems and landfills, followed by agricultural activities, coal mines, and wastewater treatment facilities. Nitrous oxide is primarily from agricultural soil management.

The fluorinated gases (HFCs, PFCs and SF6) must be included in a climate change program even though they account for less than 3 percent of total U.S. greenhouse gas emissions. Fluorinated gases are very potent greenhouse gases, several with global warming potentials thousands of times greater than that of CO2. These gases can play a larger role in addressing climate change than one would expect based on their share of the greenhouse gas inventory. The inventory is based on contribution to global warming over a 100-year time period,[5] but many of the fluorinated gases have atmospheric lifetimes much longer or much shorter than 100 years.

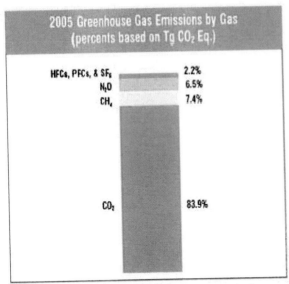

Total U.S. greenhouse gas emissions = 7,260 Million Metric Tons CO_2 Equivalent in 2005

Source: Inventory of U.S. Greenhouse Gas Emissions and Sinks. 1990-2005 (EPA, 2007).

Figure 1. U.S. Greenhouse Gas Emissions (2005).

Therefore, reducing emissions of these gases provides benefits that are not fully reflected by their contribution to the inventory. Some of these gases (e.g., HFCs) have relatively short lifetimes once emitted into the atmosphere. Reducing emissions of these short- lived gases would have a larger impact in the short run, slowing down the rate of temperature change more than reducing a comparable amount of other greenhouse gases with longer lifetimes. On the other end of the spectrum, some of these gases will stay in the atmosphere for thousands of years after they are emitted. SF6, for example, has a lifetime of 3,200 years. It has a global warming potential almost 23,000 times that of CO2 over a 100-year time period, but over a 500-year time period its global warming potential is more than 32,000 times that of CO2.[6] SF6 emitted today will contribute to global warming for centuries to come. It is also important to cover fluorinated gases in the climate change program because there are significant, cost-effective opportunities to reduce their emissions.

Economic Sectors

Direct greenhouse gas emissions are attributable to the following sectors of the economy:

- Electricity Generation (34% of U.S. greenhouse gas emissions in 2005): The emissions from this sector predominantly consist of CO_2 emissions from the combustion of fossil fuels.
- Transportation (28%):
- The emissions from this sector are predominantly CO_2 emissions from the combustion of petroleum based fuels.
- Industrial (19%):
- This sector's emissions are largely CO_2 emissions from the combustion of fossil fuels to produce steam and/or heat for industrial processes.
- Commercial (6%):
- This sector's emissions are mainly CO_2 emissions due to consumption of natural gas and petroleum products for heating, cooking, and equipment needs of businesses, governments, and other private and public organizations.
- Residential (5%):
- This sector's emissions are mainly CO_2 emissions due to the consumption of natural
- gas and petroleum products for heating and cooking needs of private homes.
- Agricultural (8%):

The emissions from this sector are primarily direct methane and nitrous oxide emissions from a variety of sources, including soil management practices.

Figure 2 shows the percentage of greenhouse gases directly emitted by each of these sectors. Figure 3 shows the primary type of sources of direct emissions from each sector.

These sectors contribute to greenhouse gas emissions in at least two ways — direct emissions (i.e., greenhouse gas emissions directly emitted by sources in that sector) and indirect emissions (e.g., CO_2 emitted as a result of electricity used by the sector, but generated outside the sector). For each sector, Figure 4 shows both the sector's direct emissions of each of the greenhouse gases and the indirect emissions from its electricity use.

We start with a strong presumption that all U.S. greenhouse gas emissions should be covered by the cap-and-trade program. Excluding from the cap-and-trade program emissions from some sectors or their sources would likely increase the burden on the covered sectors and sources to achieve a 60 to 80 percent reduction in U.S. greenhouse gas emissions. This burden on covered sectors and sources could be exacerbated if the program were designed in a way that allowed a shift of emissions from covered to uncovered sources, often referred to as "leakage." Leakage would probably occur if there are different ways of obtaining a product and only one is covered by the cap. For example, including the emissions from electricity generators in the cap, but excluding emissions of large commercial or industrial facilities, could create a financial incentive for those facilities to generate their own electricity and avoid the costs incurred by electricity generators to comply with the cap-and-trade program.

An effective cap-and-trade program requires accurate accounting for emissions. Designing a cap-and-trade program requires an understanding for each sector of the chain of economic activity associated with each type of greenhouse gas emissions and selection of one point in the chain that can be responsible for tracking the emissions and turning in allowances to cover those emissions. This is often called the "point of regulation."[7]

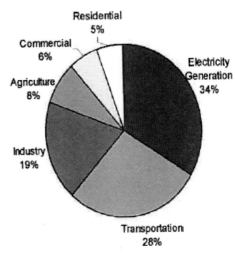

Sector/Source	2005 Emissions (MMTCO$_2$eq)
Electricity Generation	2,429.8
Transportation	2,008.9
Industry	1,352.8
Agriculture	595.4
Commercial	431.4
Residential	380.7
Total*	7,199.0

*excludes US Territories and emission sinks

MMTCO$_2$eq = Million Metric Tons Carbon Dioxide Equivalents

Source: US Environmental Protection Agency, The US Inventory of Greenhouse Gas Emissions and Sinks (2005), April 2007.

Figure 2. Direct U.S. Greenhouse Gas Emissions by Economic Sector (2005).

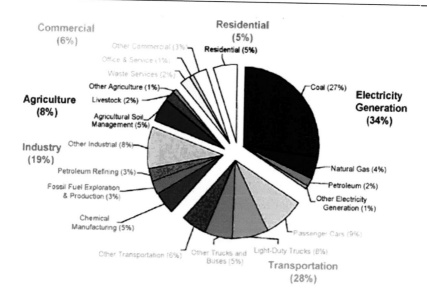

Commercial (6%)

Residential (5%)

Other Commercial (3%)

Office & Service (1%)

Waste Services (2%)

Other Agriculture (1%)

Agriculture (8%)

Livestock (2%)

Agricultural Soil Management (5%)

Industry (19%)

Other Industrial (8%)

Petroleum Refining (3%)

Fossil Fuel Exploration & Production (3%)

Chemical Manufacturing (5%)

Coal (27%)

Electricity Generation (34%)

Natural Gas (4%)

Petroleum (2%)

Other Electricity Generation (1%)

Passenger Cars (9%)

Other Transportation (6%)

Other Trucks and Buses (5%)

Light-Duty Trucks (8%)

Transportation (28%)

Source: US Environmental Protection Agency, The US Inventory of Greenhouse Gas Emissions and Sinks (2005), April 2007

Figure 3. Key Sources of Direct U.S. Greenhouse Gas Emissions by Economic Sector (2005).

The desire to cover all emissions under the cap-and-trade program must be balanced with the need to have a workable program. There are practical limits to the number and types of sources that could participate in a cap-and-trade program. Accurate monitoring and reporting are critical. An inability to determine accurately certain types of emissions may lead to the conclusion that sources of those emissions should not be required to turn in allowances equal to their emissions. If that were the case, other mechanisms to address those emissions should be explored. In addition, a sector with a very large number of sources that each have low emissions may increase the complexity and transaction costs of a cap-and-trade program. For example, for residential users (which directly emitted 5% of U.S. greenhouse gas emissions in 2005), the administrative burden (and perhaps the impossibility) of accurately determining and tracking emissions for each of the large number of small residential sources that burn natural gas, heating oil, or coal warrants their exclusion from the cap-and-trade program. In addition, transaction costs will likely be a greater administrative burden for small sources that have less reason than large sources to develop expertise in the market that will develop to trade allowances.

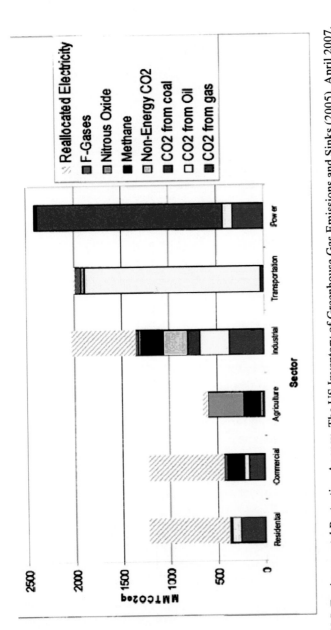

Source: U.S. Environmental Protection Agency. The US Inventory of Greenhouse Gas Emissions and Sinks.(2005), April 2007.

Figure 4. U.S. Greenhoue Gas emissions by Fuel and Economic Sector (2005).

For certain sectors with numerous small emissions sources, selecting an appropriate point of regulation might allow the sector to be included in a cap-and-trade program. To cover a sector's emissions, theoretically, the point of regulation could be set at one of several different points in the stream of commercial activities that result in greenhouse gas emissions. It could be the downstream entity that actually emits greenhouse gases (e.g., electricity generating units burning coal). It could be an upstream or midstream entity that produces, imports, processes, or transports the fuel that, when used, emits greenhouse gases (e.g., the companies supplying the coal). Thus, even though residential users should not be included in a cap-and-trade program given the administrative burden that would impose, emissions from the residential sector could be included in the cap-and-trade program by establishing the point of regulation upstream, perhaps with the fuel producers, processors, or providers. It is possible that, in the same cap-and-trade program, the point of regulation could be set at different points in the stream of commerce for different sectors (e.g., with the electricity generators for their sector and with refineries for the transportation sector). To ensure a workable program that accurately tracks emissions, setting the point of regulation upstream or midstream will require a comprehensive understanding of the chain of economic activity from fuel extraction to fuel use.[8]

The administrative burden arising from a point of regulation that would directly regulate a large number of sources in the cap-and-trade program could also be addressed by only including in the program sources above a specific threshold. For example, more than 350,000 manufacturing sources are in industries that emit CO_2 from fossil fuel combustion, but fewer than 8,000 of those sources were estimated to emit more than 10,000 tons of CO_2 in a given year.9 Theoretically, the same threshold could apply for all greenhouse gas emissions from all sectors, or different thresholds could apply for different sectors or different gases. If a threshold approach is used, care must be taken that the program does not cause a proliferation of uncovered sources just below the threshold.

In addition to the cap-and-trade program, complementary measures may be appropriate for some sectors, economic actors or types of sources. Complementary measures could either mandate or provide incentives for specific actions. They could be appropriate when certain types of emissions cannot be included in the cap-and-trade program or when the cap-and-trade program does not provide sufficient economic incentive for desired activity. For example, efficiency or other performance standards might be appropriate if some types of emissions cannot be included in the cap-and-trade program (e.g., if allowances are not required for emissions from industrial sources below a specified threshold).

Technology development or deployment may need to be encouraged through incentives for the purchase of advanced technology, or through funding for research, development, and deployment. It might also be appropriate to allow uncovered sources to opt-in to the cap-and-trade program, provided that the integrity of the cap is maintained and double counting of emission reductions does not occur. Although this chapter touches on some possible complementary measures, they will be explored more thoroughly later in this process.

Following are sector-by-sector discussions of the extent to which each of the sectors should be included in the cap-and-trade program. For each sector, the following questions are considered:

- Are there administrative reasons related to the type of sources or activities generating emissions that would make it impracticable to include them in the cap-and-trade program?
- Even if the sector generally should be included, are there administrative reasons some sources within the sector or below certain thresholds should not be included in the cap-and-trade program?
- What is the appropriate point of regulation (i.e., where should the obligation be placed to turn in allowances to cover the sector's emissions)?

Electricity Generation Sector: This sector directly emitted approximately one-third of the U.S. greenhouse gas emissions in 2005. Most of these emissions were CO_2 emissions generated from burning fossil fuels in large power plants (81% of electricity generation greenhouse as emissions come from burning coal, 13% from natural gas, and 4% from petroleum).[10] This sector includes all power generators whose primary business is the production of electricity for sale.[11] As shown in Figure 5, 72% of our electricity generation comes from burning fossil fuels, with the remainder coming from nuclear and renewable resources, including hydropower.

The cap-and-trade program will cover the electricity generation sector and establish generators as the point of regulation (i.e., the entities that must report emissions and turn in allowances sufficient to cover those emissions). This approach is based in large part on the successful Acid Rain cap-and-trade program that limits sulfur dioxide emissions from electricity generators. [12] The Acid Rain Program, which was adopted in the 1990 Clean Air Act Amendments, operates smoothly according to testimony presented to the Subcommittee. In addition to participating in the Acid Rain cap-and-trade program for sulfur dioxide emissions, electricity generators are also required to report CO_2 emissions to the Environmental Protection Agency (EPA). Accordingly, EPA and the electricity generators already have extensive experience relevant to, and much of the infrastructure necessary for, participation of this sector in a greenhouse gas cap-and-trade program. By making electricity generators the point of regulation, the cap-and-trade program will build on this existing infrastructure and experience.[13]

Although most of the units in the electricity generation sector are large units with high emissions, some units are small enough that the administrative burden of including them in the cap-and-trade program may not be warranted. One possibility is to cover units above a certain capacity.[14] For example, the Acid Rain Program applies to units attached to a generator with a nameplate capacity of 25MW or greater. This threshold would cover close to 4,900 units and 99.6% of the emissions from this sector.[15] If the threshold were set at 10 MW, it would cover an additional 2,000 units, collectively responsible for 0.3% of emissions from this sector.[16]

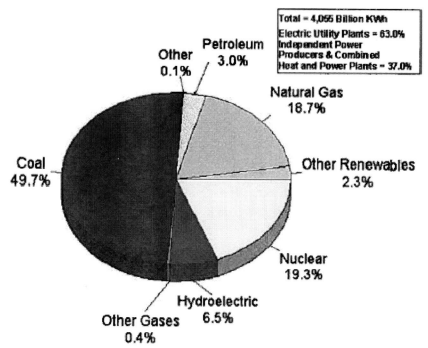

Source: Energy Information Administration, 'Electric Power Annual 2005," November 2006, pi, Attpl/www eia doe govicneaVelectriciy/epalepa stim.htmi

Figure 5. Electricity Generation by Fuel Type (2005).

Transportation Sector: This sector directly emitted 28% of the U.S. greenhouse gas emissions in 2005. The emissions from this sector come from cars (32%), light duty trucks (28%), other trucks and buses (20%) and other transportation (20%, including planes, trains, and boats).[17] Over 90% of the emissions from this sector are from burning petroleum products.

Although this sector must be included in the cap, having a downstream point of regulation (i.e., the point where the emissions occur) is not workable. Owners or operators of vehicles, the sources that actually emit greenhouse gases in this sector, are too numerous to include in a cap-and-trade program.

One possible point of regulation under a cap-and-trade program would be manufacturers of vehicles and other transportation equipment. This would require each vehicle (or other transportation equipment) manufacturer to submit allowances equal to the expected greenhouse gas emissions from the vehicles or equipment it sells. As compared to regulating consumers, this approach offers the benefit of making far fewer parties responsible for turning in allowances to cover this sector's emissions given the relatively small number of manufacturers of transportation equipment compared to users. The greenhouse gas emissions could be estimated for each vehicle or piece of equipment based on assumptions about its useful life, use patterns, and fuel consumption. Given the amount of estimation that would be required, however, this is not an ideal way of accounting for all greenhouse gas emissions from this sector. The accuracy of this method would be improved by periodically revising these assumptions.

A more promising point of regulation for this sector is upstream, i.e., refiners and importers. Adopting this point of regulation would require refiners and importers to turn in allowances to cover the carbon content of the transportation fuel they sell. Regulating refiners and importers would result in far fewer regulated entities than regulating vehicle owners or operators.[18] It would also provide for highly accurate accounting for carbon dioxide emissions because those emissions directly correspond to the carbon content of the fuel (which can be accurately determined).

If refiners and importers are designated as the "point of regulation" for the transportation sector in the cap-and-trade program, a comprehensive climate change program will also regulate motor vehicle manufacturers through efficiency or other performance standards for vehicles. Such a program will also incorporate other complementary measures such as a low carbon fuel program, and tax or other incentives to increase the use of low- emitting vehicles and to decrease vehicle usage. The design of measures to limit emissions from this sector should be informed by the lessons learned from fuel efficiency requirements for passenger vehicles, which is the only current program that essentially puts a soft cap on greenhouse gas emissions from any sector. One lesson is that the program must address all parties that contribute to emissions from this sector. Vehicles and fuels should be treated as a system, as EPA does for clean air regulations, because a vehicle's emissions depend on what goes into the car, as well as how efficient the car is. Consumer demand is also an important piece of the puzzle that must be addressed.

Industrial Sector: This sector directly emitted 19% of the United States greenhouse gas emissions in 2005. It includes manufacturing, construction and mining.[19] The types of emissions and the activities that generate them vary significantly from one industry to another. They include, for example, CO_2 emissions from fuel combustion (e.g., on-site electricity generation or steam and/or heat production for industrial processes), by-products from industrial process activities (e.g., iron and steel production, cement manufacture), and methane emissions from fossil fuel production and exploration.

Of all the sectors covered in this chapter, this is the most complex. It includes hundreds of thousands of sources. The types of facilities vary dramatically by size, type of product produced, type and amount of emissions, the process that causes the emissions, and other characteristics. Excluding this entire sector from an economy-wide program is not an option because it emits almost a fifth of the U.S. greenhouse gas emissions, but this is one of the key parts of the program that must be designed with attention to retention of manufacturing and other industrial jobs in the United States.[20]

The complexity of and regulatory issues presented by this sector are illustrated by looking just at options for covering CO_2 emissions from fossil fuel combustion from the manufacturing portion of the industrial sector (representing half of this sector's direct greenhouse gas emissions). Figure 6 shows both the number of facilities and estimated CO_2 emissions from fuel combustion for the 21 different manufacturing industries that emit CO_2 as a result of fuel combustion.[21] Some industries have a large number of facilities, but very low emissions.

If the point of regulation for the manufacturing sector's CO_2 emissions from fossil fuel combustion were placed downstream, at the source of the emissions, the cap-and-trade program could not include all of the approximately 350,000 manufacturing facilities in industries that emit CO_2 from fossil fuel combustion. Trying to include all those sources in the cap-and-trade program would add undue administrative complexity to the program, particularly since many of the sources have low emissions. Covering only sources capable of emitting above a specified threshold would dramatically reduce the number of covered entities yet still include in the cap a significant portion of the manufacturing CO_2 emissions from fossil fuel combustion. One possible threshold approach would be to cover only large emitters in high-emitting sectors (using a source-specific threshold comparable to that selected for the electricity generation sector). Figure 7 demonstrates the number of facilities above certain emissions thresholds and the total emissions from those facilities for each of the 21 manufacturing industries. A recent study estimated that 90% of the industrial sector's CO_2 emissions from fossil fuel combustion came from 6 industries (petroleum and coke, chemicals, primary metals, paper, nonmetallic mineral, and food), and 7,460 (11%) of the sources in these industries each emitted over 10,000 tons of CO_2 from fossil fuel combustion.[22] Another possible threshold approach would be to cover all large emitters in all industrial sectors. Another study estimated that approximately 95% of the manufacturing industries' CO_2 emissions from fuel combustion came from approximately 47,000 manufacturing facilities that each emitted more than 1,000 tons of CO_2, and approximately 80% came from approximately 7,800 manufacturing facilities that each emitted more than 10,000 tons of CO_2.[23]

Alternatively, if the point of regulation for manufacturers' CO_2 emissions from fossil fuel combustion were placed upstream or midstream with fuel producers, processors, or providers, the cap-and-trade program could have broader coverage of these emissions.[24] This approach would require fuel producers, processors, or providers to turn in allowances to cover the carbon content of the fuel ultimately combusted by manufacturing users. Provided there are mechanisms for distinguishing between fuel sold to manufacturing users for combustion rather than as feedstock (e.g., natural gas for manufacturing chemicals),[25] regulating fuel producers, processors or providers would provide for accurate accounting for CO_2 emissions from fossil fuel combustion because those emissions directly correspond to the carbon content of the fuel (which can be accurately determined). The feasibility of regulating manufacturers' CO_2 emissions from fossil fuel combustion by covering fuel producers, processors, or providers needs to be explored further and may depend on whether the same point of regulation is used for other sectors. One question is whether there is a point in the fuel distribution chain where it would be easy to determine and track whether fuel was being provided to a source not covered by the cap-and-trade program (e.g., an industrial user) or to a covered source (e.g., an electricity generator).

The preceding discussion focused on manufacturers' CO_2 emissions from fossil fuel combustion in part because it is the largest component of the industrial sector's emissions and in part because the available data is more robust than it is for most other types of emissions in this sector. There is good aggregate national inventory information for these other emissions, but information on emission levels from most individual facilities is generally not reported and is difficult to estimate.

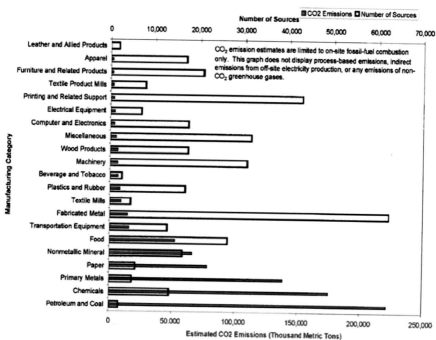

Source: Data taken from West and Pena "determining Threshholds for Mandatory Reporting of Greenhouse Gas Emissions, " Environmental Science and Technilogy, vol.37, NO. 6, 2003.

Figuire 6. NOmber of Manufgacturing Facilities and CO_2 emissions from Fossil Fuel Combustion.

Within the industrial sector, the appropriate point of regulation and the appropriate level of emissions for coverage might vary based on the nature of the emissions and the activities that generate them. CO2 emissions from fossil fuel combustion might be covered differently than methane emissions from coal mining, which might be covered differently than fluorinated gases emitted during production, either as a by-product or from the use of the gas in the industrial process. The appropriate thresholds and points of regulation for the industrial sector must take into account the potential for leakage from the electricity generation sector and the competitiveness concerns raised when some industrial facilities generate their own electricity and others (even in the same industry) buy power from other generators.

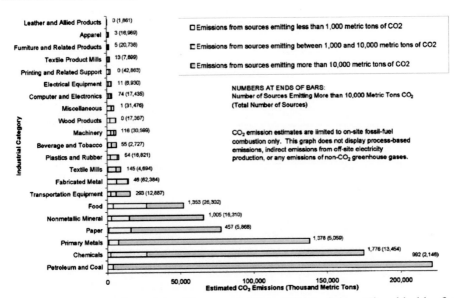

Source: Data taken from West and Pena "determining Threshholds for Mandatory Reporting of Greenhouse Gas Emissions, " Environmental Science and Technilogy, vol.37, NO. 6, 2003.

Figure 7. Large Emitters of CO2 from Fossil Fuel Combustion in each Manufacturing industry.

The complexity of this sector might make it appropriate for Congress to make initial decisions about how some industries or types of emissions should be covered, and then provide carefully circumscribed statutory authority to add other industries or types of emissions as the program matures. There may also be a role for performance standards, best management practice requirements, or other complementary measures.

Commercial Sector: This sector directly emitted 6% of U.S. greenhouse gas emissions in 2005. Approximately half of the emissions from this sector are due to consumption of natural gas and petroleum products for heating, cooking, and equipment needs of businesses, Federal, State and local Governments, and other private and public institutions.[26] This sector also includes landfills, which emit methane and account for approximately one-third of this sector's emissions, and wastewater treatment facilities. Given the variety in the types of sources and emissions in this sector, it is possible that the same approach will not work for all types of sources in this sector.

Whether the direct emissions from commercial buildings[27] could be included in the capand-trade program would depend, in part, on the point of regulation. Commercial buildings generally do not lend themselves to being the point of regulation in a cap-and-trade program given the large number of sources that each have low emissions. A 2003 study estimated that 6,000 commercial facilities emitted more than 1,000 tons CO_2 eq annually, but none emitted more than 10,000 tons CO_2 eq.[28] Another study noted that some large universities or hospitals that run large boilers for central heat might emit more than 10,000 tons of CO_2 a year.[29] Large sources, such as these types of boilers, could be included in the cap-and-trade program even though the cap-and-trade program will not include small emitters in this sector given the administrative burden that would impose.

A cap-and-trade program might be able to provide broad coverage of emissions from commercial buildings if the point of regulation were upstream or midstream, which would require fuel producers, processors, or providers to turn in allowances to cover the carbon content of the fuel that ultimately is sold to commercial buildings.[30] Using an upstream or midstream point of regulation would provide for accurate accounting for carbon dioxide emissions, which directly correspond to the carbon content of the fuel (which can be accurately determined). The feasibility of using an upstream or midstream point of regulation to cover emissions from commercial buildings needs to be explored further and may depend on whether the same point of regulation is used for other sectors. One question is whether there is a point in the fuel distribution chain where it would be easy to determine and track whether fuel ultimately would be burned by a source not covered by the cap-and-trade program (e.g., a residential user or commercial building) or to a covered source (e.g., an electricity generator).

Rather than including emissions from commercial buildings in the cap-and-trade program, it might be appropriate to reduce their emissions through building codes and efficiency or other performance standards (e.g., for furnaces).[31] If the emissions from this sector cannot generally be included in the cap-and-trade program, it might also be possible to allow commercial buildings to opt-in as a way of providing incentives for the construction of very efficient buildings, provided that this does not impair the integrity of the cap.

Approximately 10 percent of the emissions from the commercial sector come from the use of fluorinated gases, primarily HFCs, used to replace ozone depleting substances that are being phased out under the Montreal Protocol.[32] These gases are used primarily for refrigeration and air conditioning. Fluorinated gases used as substitutes for ozone depleting substances are also in the emissions inventories for the transportation, commercial, and industrial sectors. A small number of companies make fluorinated gases used as substitutes for ozone depleting substances, which should make an upstream point of regulation an efficient way to account for these gases in the cap-and-trade program.

Greenhouse gas emissions from other sources in this sector (such as landfills) generally may not lend themselves to regulation under a cap-and-trade program if there is difficulty in measuring the emissions accurately. Such sources may, however, provide significant opportunities to reduce emissions in a way that allows the reductions to be determined accurately. This could make them appropriate as a source of credits or offsets in a cap-and-trade program. For example, EPA currently operates methane programs that encourages landfills and other sources to capture gas and use it for electricity generation.[33] This program has protocols for accurately determining the resulting reduction in greenhouse gas emissions. A later White Paper will discuss the potential for using such reductions as offsets or credits as part of the capand-trade program.

Residential Sector: This sector directly emitted 5% of U.S. greenhouse gas emissions in 2005. The emissions from this sector are primarily from burning natural gas or petroleum products for heating and cooking in private homes.[34]

Inclusion of emissions from the residential sector raises essentially the same issues raised by the commercial sector. The cap-and-trade program will not regulate the residential sector's emissions with a downstream point of regulation (i.e., where the emissions actually occur) given the large number of residential sources that each have very small emissions. A cap-and-trade program might, however, be able to cover emissions from the residential sector if the point of regulation were upstream or midstream (with fuel producers or some other entity in the fuel processing and distribution chain). The feasibility of regulating this sector through fuel producers, processors, or providers needs to be explored further and may depend on the point of regulation chosen for other sectors, including the commercial sector. As with emissions from the commercial sector, it might be appropriate to address this sector's emissions through building codes and efficiency or other performance standards (e.g., for furnaces and water heaters).[35]

Agricultural Sector: This sector directly emitted 8% of U.S. greenhouse gas emissions in 2005. Approximately two-thirds of the emissions were nitrous oxide (N20), largely the result of agricultural soil management (e.g., fertilizer application) and manure management. Approximately one-third of the emissions were methane, largely from enteric fermentation (a digestive process of ruminant animals) and manure management.[36]

Greenhouse gas emissions from the agricultural sector generally do not lend themselves to regulation under a cap-and-trade program. There are a large number of sources with small individual emissions that would be impractical to measure.

A 2003 study estimated that 19,000 farms emitted more than 1,000 tons CO2 eq, but that none of those farms emitted more than 10,000 tons CO2 eq annually.[37] Accurately determining emissions is also an issue. For example, N20 released from fertilizer use cannot be measured directly by putting a monitor on the field, and there do not appear to be good proxies for measuring N20 emissions.[38]

The agricultural sector, however, does have significant opportunities to reduce emissions that may lend themselves to measurement, which could make them appropriate as a source of credits or offsets in a cap-and-trade program. For example, EPA currently operates a methane capture program that encourages large animal feeding operations to treat manure in a way that maximizes the amount of methane that could then be burned to generate electricity.[39] This program has protocols for accurately determining the resulting reduction in greenhouse gas emissions Cropland, when properly managed, can serve as a biological sink by pulling carbon out of the atmosphere. A later White Paper will discuss the potential for using such reductions as offsets or credits as part of the cap-and-trade program.

SUMMARY

- The United States needs to reduce its greenhouse gas emissions by 60 to 80 percent by 2050 to contribute to global efforts to address climate change.
- The United States needs an economy-wide, mandatory greenhouse gas reduction program.
- Primary reliance will be placed on the use of a cap-and-trade program, but complementary programs will also be needed.
- The following greenhouse gases will be included in the cap-and-trade program:

  o Carbon dioxide (CO2);
  o Methane (CH4);
  o Nitrous oxide (N20); and
  o Fluorinated Gases: Hydrofluorocarbons (HFCs), perfluorocarbons (PFCs), and sulfur hexafluoride (SF6).

- The desire to cover all greenhouse gas emissions in a cap-and-trade program must be balanced against the need to have an efficiently administered program. The inability to determine emissions (or a proxy) from sources within a given sector and/or having a large number of sources that each have low emissions may render their direct coverage by the program untenable.

- The point of regulation (i.e., the parties responsible for tracking emissions and turning in allowances) in a cap-and-trade program for any particular sector does not have to be the source that emits the greenhouse gases.
- The sectors that directly emit greenhouse gases are:

  o Electricity generation;
  o Transportation;
  o Industrial;
  o Commercial;
  o Residential; and
  o Agricultural.

- The electricity generation sector should be included in the cap-and-trade program.

  o The point of regulation should be the electricity generating facilities.
  o Only units above a specified threshold should be included in the program. The threshold could be based on generation capacity (e.g., 25 MW, as in the Acid Rain Program, or 10 MW) or on the potential annual CO_2 emissions (e.g., 10,000 tons

- The transportation sector should be included in the cap-and-trade program.

  o The most comprehensive point of regulation for the cap-and-trade program would be the refiners and importers of transportation fuel.
  o A comprehensive climate change program will also regulate motor vehicle manufacturers through efficiency or other performance standards for vehicles. Such a program will also incorporate other complementary measures such as a low carbon fuel program, and tax or other incentives to increase the use of low- emitting vehicles and to decrease vehicle usage.
- The industrial sector should be included in the cap-and-trade program.

o A large number of facilities in this sector have very low emissions and should not be directly included in the cap-and-trade program.

o Additional information is needed on the types of emissions, the activities that produce them, and the types of facilities to determine the appropriate point of regulation and threshold for coverage.

- The commercial sector's treatment in a cap-and-trade program may depend on the point of regulation and type of facility.

  o For commercial buildings, if the point of regulation is downstream (i.e., the emitters), then a threshold would be needed so that only large emitters are included in the cap-and-trade program.

  o For commercial buildings, an upstream or midstream point of regulation (i.e., fuel producers, processors or providers) would allow greater coverage of this sector's emissions, but additional information on the feasibility of this approach is needed.

  o For commercial buildings, building codes, and efficiency or other performance standards might be appropriate in addition to or instead of including this sector in the cap-and-trade program. If emissions from this sector cannot generally be addressed through the cap-and-trade program, there may be opportunities to allow commercial buildings to opt-in, provided that the integrity of the cap is maintained.

  o Fluorinated gases used as substitutes for ozone depleting substances (e.g., for refrigeration and air conditioning) should be covered in a cap-and-trade program, perhaps using the manufacturers (and importers) as the point of regulation. This same approach could apply to substitutes for ozone depleting substances used in other sectors.

  o For landfills (and perhaps other sources in this sector), an inability to measure direct emissions may preclude their inclusion in the cap. They might, however, provide opportunities for offsets and credits if emission reductions can be determined accurately.

- The residential sector's treatment in a cap-and-trade program may depend on the point of regulation.

  o A downstream point of regulation (i.e., residential users) would preclude inclusion of this sector in the cap-and-trade program because of the large number of residential users, each with low emissions.

o An upstream or midstream point of regulation (i.e., fuel producers, processors or providers) would allow broad coverage of this sector's emissions, but additional information about the feasibility of this approach is needed.

o Building codes and efficiency or other performance standards might be appropriate in addition to or instead of including this sector in the cap-and-trade program.

- The agricultural sector's direct emissions generally should not be included in the capand-trade program because of difficulties monitoring the emissions and the large number of sources each with low emissions.

o This sector may present opportunities for emission reductions that would be measurable and might then provide offset or credit opportunities.

REFERENCES

[1]   1 United States Climate Action Partnership (USCAP), "A Call to Action," at pp. 6-7. Pre-industrial concentrations of CO_2 were approximately 280 ppm.

[2]   21:PCC, "Summary for Policymakers," Climate Change 2007: The Physical Science Basis. Contribution of Working Group Ito the Fourth Assessment Report of the Intergovernmental Panel on Climate Change, 2007 at p.

[3]   For example, household appliances have a major effect on greenhouse gas emissions due to the electricity necessary to run them. Improving their energy efficiency significantly reduces greenhouse gas emissions. Nonetheless, appliance manufacturers should not be included in the cap-and-trade program for these indirect greenhouse gas emissions. That would result in double counting given that the electricity sector's emissions will be covered by the cap-and-trade program. Appliance manufacturers will, however, be required to participate in the national climate change program by meeting energy efficiency standards, which will achieve significant reductions without double counting. For example, the appliance and lighting efficiency standards in H.R. 3221, the House energy bill, are projected to reduce more than 2.5 billion tons CO2eq cumulatively through 2030. (Note that direct emissions from the process of manufacturing appliances will need to be addressed consistently with other industrial sector emissions.)

[4]   Greenhouse gases vary in the extent to which they cause global warming and in the amount of time they last in the atmosphere. A ton of methane does not have the same effect on the earth's temperature as a ton of CO_2. For ease of comparison, the accepted international and scientific convention is to compare greenhouse gases based on their contribution to global warming over a 100-year period compared to the contribution of CO_2. Thus, greenhouse gas emissions are reported as tons of CO_2-equivalent (or tons CO_2eq). (E.g., 1 ton of CH_4 = 21 tons CO_2eq).

[5]   See n. 4. Although the comparison over a 100-year time period is a useful convention for developing climate change policy, at times it is helpful to have a deeper understanding of how different gases contribute to global warming.

[6]   6IPCC, Climate Change 2001: The Scientific Basis. Contribution of Working Group I to the Third Assessment Report of the Intergovernmental Panel on Climate Change, 2001 at Table 6.7, p. 389

[7]   7The "point of regulation" refers to the type of entity that is obligated to turn in allowances to cover emissions. Depending on the economic activity producing the greenhouse gas emissions, the point of regulation could be set "upstream" with the producer, "downstream" with the emitter, or somewhere in-between in the stream of commerce that moves the fuel from the producer to the emitter ("midstream").In many regulatory programs, the point of regulation is the source that actually emits the pollutant. This is referred to as "downstream" regulation because the emitter is the end of the stream of commerce that results in the emissions. This is the point of regulation used in the Acid Rain Trading Program, in which electricity generators are required to report their sulfur dioxide (SO_2) emissions and then turn in the number of allowances that equals their emissions.Under a cap-and-trade program, other points of regulation are possible, particularly to address greenhouse gas emissions from fossil fuel combustion. This is because the amount of carbon in fuel (e.g., in coal, gas, oil) determines the amount of CO_2 emissions that will result when the fuel is burned (unless the CO_2 is sequestered, which can be accounted for separately). Therefore, instead of setting the point of regulation with the emitter, the emissions could also be tracked and covered by setting the point of regulation with the company that produces a fuel, and that producer would be required to turn in allowances equal to the CO_2 emissions that will result when the fuel it sells is eventually burned. This is generally referred to as "upstream" regulation. Upstream regulation may also be appropriate for a large percentage of fluorinated gas emissions.

[8]   A program with an upstream or midstream point of regulation would need to ensure appropriate treatment of imported and exported fuel so that covered fuel would be that fuel combusted in the United States.

[9]   West, Tristam O. and Pefia, Naomi, "Determining Thresholds for Mandatory Reporting of Greenhouse Gas Emissions," Environmental Science & Technology, Vol. 37, No. 6, 2003 at Table 1.

[10] For this and other sectors, this chapter generally describes the types of sources and emissions that comprise the majority of the sector's emissions. This description, however, is not exhaustive. For example, the electricity sector emissions also include other types of emissions, such as SF_6 emissions from the transmission and distribution of electricity and nitrous oxide emissions from fossil fuel combustion. For more detailed information on each sector's emissions, see US Environmental Protection Agency, The US Inventory of Greenhouse Gas Emissions and Sinks (2005), April 2007.

[11] Emissions from electricity generated primarily for the generator's own use (e.g., a resort that generates its own electricity) are not included in the electricity generation sector. Rather, they are included in that generator's sector (e.g., in the commercial sector for emissions from a resort).

[12] Depending on their geographic location, power plants may also be subject to a nitrogen oxide trading program, a mercury trading program, and/or a sulfur dioxide trading program tighter than the acid rain program.

[13] There are alternative ways to include electricity generation emissions in a greenhouse gas cap-and-trade program. For example, the electricity generation sector could be covered by using the carbon content of fuel as a proxy for carbon emissions instead of relying on monitored emissions. Coal, natural gas, and oil producers, processors or providers could be the point of regulation (rather than electricity generators) and would be required to turn in allowances based on the carbon content and amount of fuel they sold. Such a system would need to provide credits or some other mechanism of accounting for carbon captured and sequestered as part of the electricity generation process.

[14] Another possibility is to cover this sector based on capacity to emit CO_2 above a specified level. In 2002, all of the electricity generation sector's CO_2 emissions from fossil fuel combustion were from approximately 2,220 facilities (note that "facilities" are different than "units" used in the text) that each emitted more than 1,000 tons, and 99.9% came from approximately 1,600 facilities that each emitted more than 10,000 tons. Nicholas Institute for Environmental Policy Solutions, Size Thresholds for Greenhouse Gas

Regulation: Who Would be Affected by a 10,000-ton CO2Emissions Rule?, September 2007 at p. 4.

[15] Environmental Protection Agency, eGRID2006 Version 2.1 (April 30, 2007).

[16] ibid.

[17] See n. 10.

[18] 149 refineries cover 90% of the refined products sold in the United States. Energy Information Agency, Form- 820, Annual Refinery Report (ht tp : / /www eia . doe . gov/oss / forms . html # top).

[19] See n. 10.

[20] For example, the mechanisms for distributing allowances and addressing developing countries' obligationsregarding their emissions could play critical roles in how a U.S. climate program affects the industrial sector.

[21] The findings presented in Figure 6 are consistent with a more recent study. Nicholas Institute, September 2007.

[22] Nicholas Institute, 2007 at Table 5.

[23] West and Pena, 2003 at Table 3. A more recent study found that about 8,000 manufacturing facilities (2.3% of all United States manufacturing facilities) each emitted more than 10,000 tons of CO_2 from fossil fuel combustion and accounted for 85% of the manufacturing industry's CO_2 emissions from fossil fuel combustion. Nicholas Institute, 2007 at Table 5.

[24] See n. 8.

[25] One possibility is information currently provided to the Energy Information Administration regarding end uses of fossil fuels.

[26] See n. 10.

[27] This chapter will use "commercial buildings" to describe the sources of direct emissions from heating, cooking, and equipment needs of businesses, Federal, State and local Governments, and other private and public institutions. Common types of commercial buildings are office buildings, universities, hospitals, hotels, and resorts.

[28] West and Pena, 2003 at Table 3.

[29] Nicholas Institute, September 2007 at p. 4.

[30] See n. 8.

[31] Such programs, which would not necessarily be federal programs, could also be adopted in addition to a cap-andtrade program as a way of ensuring that the market provides high efficiency products for commercial buildings facing increases in fuel costs. Building codes and efficiency or other performance standards could also be used to reduce the commercial buildings' indirect emissions from their use of electricity.

[32] The gases that are being replaced are even more potent greenhouse gases
      than the fluorinated gases. EPA, Achievements in Stratospheric Ozone
      Protection: Progress Report, April 2007 at p. 33. Although chemicals being
      phased out under the Montreal Protocol contribute to global warming, they
      are not addressed in the U.S. greenhouse gas emissions inventory because
      they are already addressed internationally under the Montreal Protocol.
      EPA, The U.S. Inventory of Greenhouse Gas Emissions and Sinks (2005),
      April 2007 at p. ES-2.

[33] EPA, "Methane-to-Markets." http://www.epa.gov/methanetomarkets/

[34] See n. 10

[35] Such programs, which would not necessarily be Federal programs, could be
      adopted in addition to a cap-and-trade program as a way of ensuring that the
      market provides high efficiency products for residential customers facing
      increases in fuel costs. Building codes and performance or other efficiency
      standards could also be used to reduce the residential sector's indirect
      emissions from its use of electricity

[36] See n. 10.

[37] West and Pena, 2003 at Table 2.

[38] Differences in fertilizers, soil conditions, and farming practices make it
      difficult to measure or report on factors that could be used as a proxy for
      measuring emissions. This is in contrast to the carbon content of fuel, which
      is a good proxy for the amount of carbon that will be released when the fuel
      is burned.

[39] EPA, "Methane-to-Markets." http://www.epa.gov/methanetomarkets/

In: Constructing Climate Change Legislation... ISBN 978-1-60692-986-5
Editor: Gerald P. Overhauser, pp. © 2009 Nova Science Publishers, Inc.

Chapter 5

MEMORANDUM

TO: Members, Committee on Energy and Commerce
FROM: Rick Boucher, Chairman
Subcommittee on Energy and Air Quality
John D. Dingell, Chairman Committee on Energy and Commerce
SUBJECT: Climate Change Discussion Draft Legislation

Today we are pleased to release a discussion draft of climate change legislation. This draft is the culmination of nearly two years of intensive work on climate change by the Committee and marks an important step in our ongoing efforts to address this increasingly serious problem.

Since the Committee began its examination of the issue in January 2007, our work has been predicated on the belief that a thorough, deliberative, and purposeful examination of the facts would yield the best result. To that end, we have held 27 hearings, released four white papers on different aspects of climate policy, conducted numerous workshops, and received thousands of pages of written responses to our letters and questions for the record. It must be noted that in the midst of this activity, the committee also took the lead in drafting and passing energy legislation that greatly aids our task on climate change. We enacted a landmark 40 percent increase in Corporate Average Fuel Economy (CAFE) standards; passed energy efficiency measures that will remove 10 billion tons of carbon dioxide from the atmosphere by 2030; and passed a sweeping overhaul of the Renewable Fuels Standard (RFS) that will speed the development of low carbon biofuels while lessening our dependency on foreign oil.

Since January 2007, the debate over climate change has evolved dramatically, beginning with groundbreaking reports released by the International Panel on

Climate Change, which affirmatively settled the question of whether human activity is contributing to global warming In addition, in the absence of Federal action, some 24 states and several regional organizations have moved towards regulation of greenhouse gases. While the States should be lauded for their progressive stance in addressing the problem, their actions, if not properly coordinated and directed and accompanied by Federal action, could be disruptive to interstate commerce and counterproductive to the goal of limiting national greenhouse gas emissions. Finally, the Supreme Court added another layer of complexity and urgency to our task when it ruled in Massachusetts v. EPA, that CO_2 is a pollutant, with the almost certain consequence that the Environmental Protection Agency (EPA) will in the near term regulate CO_2 emissions under the existing Clean Air Act (CAA), unless Congress enacts a regulatory statute.

Politically, scientifically, legally, and morally, the question has been settled: regulation of greenhouse gases in the United States is coming We believe that elected and accountable representatives in the Congress, not the Executive Branch, should properly design that regulatory program. The only remaining question is what form that regulation will take.

The discussion draft begins to answer that question with a deliberate, thoughtful policy that will preserve economic growth while protecting our environment. The discussion draft would establish an economy-wide cap on emissions of greenhouse gases. In the early years of the program, caps would be set at a level that is realistically achievable to ensure that firms are able to adjust gradually. By 2050, emissions from covered sources would be reduced to 80 percent below 2005 levels, ensuring the substantial reductions necessary to contribute to stabilizing global concentrations of greenhouse gases. The program's trading mechanisms provide firms with maximum flexibility and establish incentives for the development of new energy and abatement technologies. Costs to firms and consumers are managed in several ways, including: the availability of cost-effective, high quality offsets; the ability of firms to access a special "reserve" of emission allowances when prices rise; and an aggressive program to improve energy efficiency and deploy clean technologies, including carbon capture and sequestration.

The discussion draft presents four options concerning how emission allowances might be allocated to firms, States, consumers, and other areas. Provisions for strong market oversight and the protection of American jobs are also included. Further details on the discussion draft are attached.

The Committee on Energy and Commerce brings to this discussion a useful and unique perspective. The Committee authored the sulfur dioxide, or acid rain, emissions trading program contained in the 1990 Clean Air Act Amendments that is the model for current and proposed capand-trade programs for greenhouse gas emissions. For example, the European Union in major respects modeled its CO2 Emissions Trading System on our SO2 cap-and-trade program. The Committee also has extensive expertise in developing and overseeing auction programs that generate revenue for the taxpayer, such as telecommunications spectrum auctions.

It is noteworthy that the Committee drafted and took the lead in passing the first three significant clean air statutes which became law in 1970, 1977, and 1990. These measures resulted from bipartisan cooperation and enjoyed broad bipartisan support in both Houses of the Congress. They also resulted from an extensive consultation with clean air advocates and the industries proposed to be regulated by the legislation. We seek to follow that successful model in constructing a climate change regulatory bill.

Our goal is to craft a bill that can be enacted quickly and lead to regulations that can be implemented with a minimum of administrative or legal impediments. Achieving that goal will require us to assemble a bipartisan coalition that bridges legitimate policy disagreements rooted in regional economics and other factors that cross party lines. To that end, we welcome the active participation of all of our colleagues in both parties. Regrettably, the Bush Administration and the Committee's Republican leadership have yet to engage in a constructive dialogue on how to structure a mandatory greenhouse gas reduction program. We would prefer to have the benefit of their good ideas, their active work in refining the legislation, and their cooperation in passing it into law. The demise of the climate change bill in the Senate earlier this year underscores the need to reach a broad bipartisan consensus.

What we are releasing today is a discussion draft. It contains clear policies in areas where we have learned enough to set forth recommendations, though those recommendations will certainly benefit from additional refinement based on comments from Members and interested stakeholders. hi other areas we believe we need further deliberation. Reaching a consensus on a national approach to addressing climate change will be difficult under the best of circumstances. Reaching consensus if people are unwilling to engage in discussion of difficult issues will be impossible. For that reason, this discussion draft acknowledges different views by presenting options representing a range of potential ways to address issues such as allocations and treatment of state motor vehicle standards.

The discussion draft is guided by several core principles:

1. Emission levels and timetables should be realistic and scientifically-driven. Emission caps in the program's early years, which are set at the upper end of the ranges recommended by United States Climate Action

Partnership (USCAP) in its Call to Action, would allow the economy to adjust to new prices for carbon while simultaneously creating marketplace incentives to reward innovations in technology and greenhouse gas mitigation. The draft follows the upper USCAP range in the years between program implementation and the time we anticipate that carbon capture and sequestration technologies will become available for wide deployment. Thereafter, the reduction requirements become much more stringent and track quickly to the lower end of the ranges recommended by USCAP. In doing so, the discussion draft would require the substantial reductions necessary to contribute to stabilizing global concentrations of greenhouse gases. We have worked within the bounds of USCAP's proposal because it represents a consensus among business, environmental, and other groups.

2. Energy efficiency and development of clean energy technologies are vital greenhouse gas reduction strategies that also have economic benefits for the Nation. A substantial number of allowances are directed to programs to improve energy efficiency and deploy low, or zero, carbon technologies. The discussion draft would also drive increases in building and appliance efficiencies. Firms and consumers stand to gain substantial savings from further improvements in energy efficiency, which would reduce the overall cost of the program. The discussion draft's bonus allowance provisions would encourage the deployment of advanced technologies like carbon capture and sequestration, along with zero-carbon generation from wind, solar, and other renewable resources.

3. Limiting the cost of the program will protect U.S. jobs, consumers, and industry. The discussion draft relies on a cap-and-trade program, improvements in energy efficiency, and the use of offsets as the primary mechanisms to reduce the cost of greenhouse gas reductions. In addition, firms would be able to bank and borrow allowances, and a "strategic reserve" would release additional allowances should prices rise too high. Finally, the discussion draft would provide for strict oversight of the carbon market to ensure its efficient operation without market manipulation.

4. Everyone must do their fair share to reduce emissions, and all levels of Government have a role to play. The discussion draft would create an economy-wide program to reduce greenhouse gas emissions. It would rely on Federal-State-local partnerships to reduce emissions by providing allowances and preserving authority for many State and local regulatory programs.

5. Proper allocation of allowances is critical to a cap-and-trade program, but broad consensus is lacking. The discussion draft contains four options for allocating allowance value. All would provide substantial allowance value for energy efficiency, clean technology deployment, and low income protection. The options differ in the amount of allowance value they give to covered sectors, to other programs for reducing greenhouse gas emissions, to programs to adapt to climate change, and to consumers. In recognition of the impossibility of allocating allowances now for the next four decades, the draft bill would auction all of the allowances from 2026 on and send the fees paid on a per capita basis back to American citizens unless Congress reauthorized the bill. The insertion of this provision is designed to motivate a Congressional reauthorization prior to 2026.

6. Implementation matters. Throughout the discussion draft, provisions have been added to simplify the administration of, and compliance with, the program. Particular care was given to crafting various provisions to minimize the creation of new institutions, streamline regulatory development and program implementation, and build upon existing institutional expertise. In addition, rather than layering a program to reduce greenhouse gases on top of the existing Clean Air Act, the draft bill directly modifies existing authority so there would be one sensible, comprehensive program.

We want to acknowledge the efforts of several members of the committee who contributed valuable policy ideas that are reflected in this draft: Representative Baldwin for her work on a greenhouse gas registry, Representatives Inslee and Doyle for their ideas on protecting energy intensive industries, Representative Markey for his ideas on carbon market oversight, Representative Inslee for his work on black carbon, and Representative Solis for her suggestions for protecting low-income consumers.

Finally, in presenting this discussion draft, we would offer two observations.

While this draft presents a regulatory framework for reducing greenhouse gas emissions, regulation alone will never achieve our reduction targets. We will need massive and unprecedented investments in both existing and innovative technologies that do not contribute to climate change. For example, we will need rapid development and deployment of carbon capture and sequestration (CCS) technology and increased production of electricity from nuclear, wind, solar, tidal, geothermal, and other sources of power to help meet our projected electricity load growth and permit economic expansion. To that end, we expect to quickly pass the bipartisan "Carbon Capture and Storage Early Deployment Act" offered earlier this year.

Second, we do not pretend or guarantee that a successful climate change policy will be without cost or adjustment. Our task as legislators is to see that it is accomplished in the most effective and minimally disruptive fashion.

With regard to climate change mitigation, we have known for some time where we want to go: a reduction in greenhouse gas emissions of 80 percent below 2005 levels by 2050. With this discussion draft we propose some ways to get there. We hope that all interested parties will take the time to review the draft and provide us with detailed commentary so that we may begin the next session of Congress more informed and better able to move legislation quickly.

We look forward to receiving your comments and working with you.

INDEX

D

E

F

G

T

U

V